Lightly Poached

A childhood memoir of village, school and farm life in the Forest of Dean

by Danny Haines

Published by
Parva Dene Publications

Lightly Poached

By the same author:

Shear Magic

Lightly **Poached**

A childhood memoir of village, school and farm life in the Forest of Dean

Copyright: Danny Haines 2003

British Library Cataloguing-in-Publication Data.
A catalogue record for this book is available from the British Library

ISBN 0-9543024-1-9

All rights reserved. No part of this publication may be reproduced, stored in a retrieval system or transmitted in any form or by any means, electronic, mechanical, photocopying, recording or otherwise without the written permission of the publisher.

Published by
Parva Dene Publications
Broadlands, Farm Road, Ruardean Woodside,
Gloucestershire GL17 9XL

Design, typesetting and origination by
Artytype, 6 Kings Buildings, Hill Street, Lydney,
Gloucestershire GL15 5HE

Printed by
MD Jenkins, 53/54 Lydney Industrial Estate, Harbour Road,
Lydney, Gloucestershire GL15 4EJ

Lightly Poached

Contents

Acknowledgements
Foreword

Chapter 1	The hooded crows	13
Chapter 2	If the cap fits	27
Chapter 3	The linesman's error	41
Chapter 4	A good head of steam	55
Chapter 5	Running the gypsy gauntlet	65
Chapter 6	Dick Turpin rides again	77
Chapter 7	Bottled tea and school dinners	87
Chapter 8	Names and addresses please	97
Chapter 9	Slippery as an eel	111
Chapter 10	Going against the tide	129
Chapter 11	Blue hands and tasty trout	139
Chapter 12	Billy was frothing at the mouth	151
Chapter 13	Hair like a bird's nest	163
Chapter 14	The cowshed meeting	173

Lightly Poached

Acknowledgements

I am indebted to my brother Tony, sister-in-law Pat and cousin Molly for their help in recalling some of the events from the 50's; invariably they were able to fill in any gaps in my memory. In addition I would like to thank Royston Mills for loaning me many of the photographs from his superb archive, and also for a brief glimpse back to the Yalu POW camp.

A special mention also goes to Ade Haines and John Powell for their enthusiastic design and development work.

My final thank-you again goes to Bernard Kear for his wonderful illustrations. His work is inspirational and no-one else seems to capture the atmosphere of the 1950's the way he does.

I have changed the names on just a few of the pranks where I thought the participants would wish to remain anonymous. I sincerely hope that the use of schoolboy nicknames does not cause undue embarrassment, especially where they have been quietly and successfully discarded for quite some time.

I have told the stories and pieces of conversation as accurately as I can recall them; if I have the odd name wrong or missed someone out, please forgive me. In a few sad instances, some of the participants are no longer with us, but I do hope their surviving family members can still enjoy reading about the way things once were.

Lightly Poached

Foreword

I was born in Littledean. It is a small village which in ancient times acted as a gateway between the wild Forest of Dean uplands and the more undulating farmland leading down to the River Severn. Records of the village go back to just after the Norman conquest and there was habitation a long time before that. And, back in 1956 when you looked at some of the old-stagers from Sheep's Head Row, you could be excused for thinking they were of a similar vintage!

The motte-and-bailey, or Roman Camp as it is called locally, sits high on a hill to the east of the village and dates back to the late 11th century; while Dean Hall, although undergoing various extensions and modifications over the years, has archaeology dating back to the Saxon and Roman periods. It was said to be the scene of fighting in the Civil War when two Royalist officers, Colonel Congreve and Captain Wigmore, were killed by Roundhead soldiers. St Ethelbert's church goes back to the 14th century and, a little further down the road, is the Gaol, one of four identical bridewells built in the county in 1791.

The main Gloucester to Cinderford road meandered its way through the village and, every morning at around half past eight, the Red and White double-decked bus bulged with youngsters on their way to the secondary schools in Cinderford. When the

• *Broad Street, Littledean c1910.*   *Photo courtesy of County Records Office*

- *Broad Street, Littledean – long before cars.*   Photo courtesy of Roy Mills

last pick-up was made by the George Hotel it was standing room only; the conductor certainly had his work cut out to make sure everyone had bought a ticket.

Heavily laden lorries struggled up the steep 'new road' to Sawney's Lookout; it was not unusual for some of the more daring boys to grab hold of the back of a slow moving one to get their push-bikes towed to the top of the hill. It was a risky business, especially if the driver caught sight of you in his rear mirror and slammed on his brakes.

Tom Davis ran the Post Office in the middle of the village and, on the opposite side of the road, there was Mrs Jefferies' hardware shop and Jack Davis' grocery shop. Jack Snr had for many years put a lot of effort into organising an annual flower show which was always very popular. Mrs Wiggle had a small sweet-shop down on Church Street near our old home on the Cross, and Mort Giles, the butcher, operated from a shop next to the King's Head, the other pub in the village. I was always fascinated to watch Mort sharpen a knife; he would whip the blade along alternate sides of a steel faster than the eye could follow. Danny Beard was a genial and portly figure who ran a fish and chip shop next to the George Hotel; it was a very popular place after a game of skittles and a few pints. Danny was a likeable chap and I remember how obliging he was, even to bits of kids like myself.

Every August the carnival procession paraded along Broad Street accompanied by bands, numerous floats and shrieking youngsters. Yes, crowning the carnival queen was a big event in those days, it ranked alongside the sheep sale when it came to pulling in a big crowd.

Littledean Rovers were doing quite well; they had two sides and the young men of the village turned out every week come sleet, rain or sunshine. Nearly all the players lived in the village and, even if they didn't already drink together, they still knew each other very well. Team spirit was never a problem, they all pulled together. However, the rules in football regarding the protection of goalkeepers were open to interpretation back then, and the Rovers had sustained injuries in that department. Ray Hawkins had been playing at centre forward earlier in the season but suddenly found himself pressed into action between the posts.

In Cinderford, Percy Drew had a special deal going, a mere 40/- for a pair of men's sheepskin lined boots. Nearby was the Royal Union pub, a building with a limited future if the talk of pulling it down was to be believed. There was a dance held at the Miners Welfare Hall most Saturday nights. Regular fist fights took place, either inside the Hall or outside on the steps, when the young men of the district took on any outsiders who they believed were just there to eye up their women.

Further afield, up on Ruardean Hill, our old headmaster, Wilf Meek, was in the news for his fine performances on the cricket field. Just across the valley at Howle Hill, the motorbike scrambles were a major attraction. It was nothing to get a crowd of 6-7,000 people there on a fine day; people loved to enjoy themselves out in the open air.

Men earned their living locally on farms, or travelled to find work in factories or down the mines. The Forest had a long history of mining. The iron ore and most of the quarries had long been worked out and now the dreadful conditions were endured by many as they toiled to fetch out in excess of 11,000 tons of coal from the pits every week.

Littledean itself was surrounded by farms and woodland, much of it hilly and rocky. It was an ideal playground for youngsters, and we did have such a wonderful time in those halcyon days. In the holidays and on weekends we would be up trees, on ponds or sliding down a steep bank on a piece of cardboard. And, although we were free to do more or less what we wanted, there was no need to worry, we always got back home safe and sound – eventually!

Lightly Poached

Chapter One
Late Summer 1956

They looked like hooded crows. All wore grey suits with jet black gowns and expressions to match. East Dean Grammar School was not a welcoming place on September 4th 1956. The teaching staff were seated on a high stage at one end of the Gymnasium. They were arranged with the most senior in the middle of the front row; the others, to the left and right, were in a kind of pecking order and the new staff were tucked in at the back.

There were about 90 new pupils and we were all pushed down to the very front. The more senior pupils were stood towards the back of the Gym. It was an intimidating atmosphere to be a 'new boy' sandwiched in between the crows and the school-yard bullies at the back.

The Headmaster was 'Tim' Saunders, an elderly and rather frail looking old gentleman. He too came from Littledean. He lived in the Red House, a building with a very chequered history indeed. It stood at the foot of Littledean Hill and by the side of the Ruffitt Lane. In distant times, that narrow, winding lane was the main road connecting the village to the Forest of Dean and its iron ore and other resources.

The Red House was originally a guard tower, or keep, built some time after the Norman conquest to protect the villagers against raiders from the Forest and South Wales. They were rough sods by any measure and some of them still are. Anyway, the house became a residential property some time before the 16th century, when the well-to-do Brayne family occupied it. However, they fell on hard times a century later and the Red House became a pin-making works. Times also worsened for the residents of Littledean and, by the 19th century, the building became the village workhouse.

It was in 1834 when a ten year-old boy left an account of a dastardly deed. An old miser was murdered and his body carried to the workhouse. Two suspects were then taken from the Gaol and escorted there by the constable. It was widely believed at the time if a murderer touched the corpse of his victim, it would bleed! A sizeable crowd, including the young boy, accompanied the constable and the two suspects, eager to see justice done. The corpse did not bleed on that occasion however, and we do not know what became of the suspects.

Flanking Tim up on the stage were Miss Hazell, the senior Mistress, together with Messrs Allott, Aveston and Jones. I knew then, just by looking at those chalk-covered disciplinarians, that the next five years were going to be really tough.

Plink, plink went the keys of an old piano located just in front of the stage. Miss Protheroe was not put off easily. Her elbows and knees started to move with a strange, passionate fury as she beat a tune out of the reluctant instrument.

"Tall and strong is our Forest tree,
And our woodland ways are fair to see...."

The collective voice of the assembled pupils boomed out the opening lines of the school song. To me and 89 other new starters, it was just confirmation we had arrived in Bedlam.

Morning assembly was a stand-up affair, at least it was for all the pupils. After umpteen verses of the school song, Miss Protheroe fell back exhausted. One of the male teachers rose to his feet and started reading out names and class numbers.

"Andrews, David........2A

"Beddis,.........."

I stopped listening for a moment and looked slowly around the Gym. It was a huge building, two sides of which consisted mainly of glass, this was protected by wooden climbing bars which resembled a series of wide ladders, whose rungs were only a few inches apart. Huge climbing ropes were suspended from the roof structure and their ends tucked into the top of the climbing bars. At the front of the Gym, just in front of the stage, were various sized vaulting horses and springboards. I closed my eyes and thought of how easy life had seemed an hour earlier as I walked along the George Lane with my brand new, but empty satchel slung over my shoulder. I had picked blackberries from the overgrown hedgerow and ate them as I walked. By the time I got to the bus-stop at the Kings Head, my tongue was a dark shade of purple.

"Come on 'Jammer'", I yelled to David James who seemed to be dawdling down Silver Street in a dreamlike state.

"What's the hurry", came the nonchalant reply.

I looked him up and down. He was wearing long trousers and looked very smart.

I only had short trousers on and the rest of my clothes only fitted where it touched. Mother was not much into fashion or such niceties; being hard-wearing and modestly priced were a lot higher on her agenda.

You could hear the bus coming from miles away. The old Red and White double-decked vehicle groaned after every gear change up Church Street, until finally, it came around the corner and into sight. It was packed already.

"How are we supposed to get on that?" snorted David.

"Well I 'ent walking....so there".

It wasn't really a case of 'after you'. Boys and girls fought side by side to get on the bus. Eventually the conductor moved some older boys away from the door; they had been hogging the best spot for a quick exit but were making it difficult for everyone else to get on.

The conductor certainly earned his money. He had to remember who had gone upstairs, who had already paid, and who was hiding to avoid paying. The strange thing was that he rarely missed anyone, because on the rare occasion he did, the lucky lad bragged about it all day long.

I opened my eyes again; the teacher on the stage was still droning on.

"Griffiths, Angela Mary.......2C

Haines, Daniel Henry.........2A"

"What happened to 1A?", I thought to myself.

I discovered later there was no 1A, 1B or 1 anything, the class numbers just started at 2. It made no sense at all to me, especially when I later discovered there was a Lower and an Upper class 5. However, as soon as that first assembly came to a merciful end, I made my way uncertainly to my allocated classroom. There I made a spirit-sapping discovery. For the next five years I was to be known as HAINES. All the teachers referred to boys by their surname only. There were eight 'Davids' in my class so perhaps in a way it was just as well. Even the girls in the class called me Haines.

"Oh my God", I thought, " how will I ever get through this?"

Teachers had always been so friendly in the past, I had always been called Danny, people had liked me. But now I sensed that I was a lump of meat known as Haines, and at that stage we had not had our first PE lesson!

Later in the morning, armed with a timetable for the term, I left the comparative safety of my form room when the bell sounded. I made my way to Room 3 for a maths lesson. What I hadn't anticipated was that the whole school changed rooms at the same time. 450 pupils, ranging from spotty little kids like me up to great, hulking 6th-formers, all rampaged up and down the main corridor at the same time. Being small, frightened and lost was something of a disadvantage. By the time I reached Room 3, I was scragged and battered. I crept in and sat down as near the back as I could get.

After a brief recap on arithmetic and the like, the maths teacher moved on to new ground.

"How many of you have heard of algebra?"

Hands shot up all around me. I kind of half raised mine hoping like hell he wouldn't ask me anything about it. My brother Tony had left East Dean two years earlier and, although he had totally cobbled up his final exams, he did try to explain what algebra was. It should be remembered that Tony had been expected to help out on the farm whenever needed, and his academic achievement had suffered because of it.

"It is when they use letters instead of numbers", he had told me knowledgeably, "each letter has a numerical value….that's all".

Well that had seemed simple enough to me, so I watched the master write on the blackboard. The chalk screeched so badly at times it set my teeth on edge. He had written $A=B+C$. He then turned to the class and said, "if $B=2$ and $C=3$, what is the value of A?"

Hands shot up all round me again, but I was far too busy writing $B=2$ and $C=3$ on my ruler with a Biro. He pointed to Wendy Evans, a classmate from Littledean Primary school.

"Please sir, five sir".

"Very good, and if $B=3$ and $C=7$ then what is the new value of A?"

I looked down at my brand new wooden ruler. The deep indentation of $B=2$ and $C=3$ could not be erased. I felt like a jackass and cursed Tony and his oversimplified explanation of algebra. I glanced at my watch and realised we were near to lunch-break. That at least would give me a chance for me to tie up with Royston Wellington and 'Jammer', two familiar faces from Littledean.

The bell went and, after a couple of minutes delay to reinforce time disciplines, we were released for lunch. I dropped my satchel off in my form room and ran out into the boys' yard. The new starters all stuck out like sore thumbs. Most of us were in short, grey-flannel trousers for a start, then there were the brand new, navy blue blazers and badly knotted ties. Then I spotted Royston, he was being held up against a wall by two older boys and he didn't look as if he was enjoying it very much. I wasn't sure what it was all about, so I kept out of the way until they let him go.

"What did they want?", I enquired nervously.

"They want to know your name and that", he replied, loosening his tie to prevent slow strangulation. The broad red, blue and yellow diagonal stripes now had an odd corrugated look. Just then I felt my feet leave the ground.

"What's your name?", snarled a boy whose blond wavy hair bounced as he kneed me in the groin to speed up my reply.

"Haines", I croaked with my tie yanked up the back of my left ear.

"Where are you from Haines?"

"Littledean......."

"If I have any trouble from you....you'll wish you'd stayed there....right", said his mate with another application of the knee.

I had just met Gordon Watson and one of his Lydbrook cronies. I nodded, quite terrified of the whole place, the teachers, the older boys, the prefects and even the buildings. This ritual went on for a few days until every older boy knew all the new starters. I was just ten years old, the youngest pupil in the whole school; what a welcome to East Dean!

Home was Greenway Farm. It was 52 acres of mainly arable land located about a mile from the village of Littledean. My Mother and Father, together with myself and my two older brothers, Dave and Tony, had taken the plunge into farming back in 1950.

My late Grandparents, George and Kath Leadbeater, had raised their three daughters, Win, Kath and Alice on the farm. They had owned it up until their deaths in the mid 1930's, after which it had been leased out to the Watts family until we decided to move back in.

George had been a bit of a devil in his time and loved to have a few pints. He would toddle off up to the pub on a Saturday night and have a damn good session before staggering back home. The last 100 yards down past the Cherry tree to the farmhouse was badly rutted and totally unlit. Invariably he would end up in the hedge.

"Kath......Kath.....", he would shout to his long suffering spouse.

Eventually she would hear him and come to the gate.

"George?.....where are you?"

"Do you still love me Kath?" he would ask in a hopelessly drunken voice.

"Yes dear", would come the dutiful reply.

"Then come up 'ere and get me out of these bloody brambles!".

Alice, who was later to become my mother, had left home in 1930 to get married, so the return some 20 years later had been a very emotional homecoming for her.

Most of the meadows had names that had survived for as long as any one could remember. However, old maps showed there had been some changes since the early 19th century. The Apple Meadow was originally named Hopewell; however, it is possible that the Forest tendency to abbreviate words resulted in Hopewell becoming

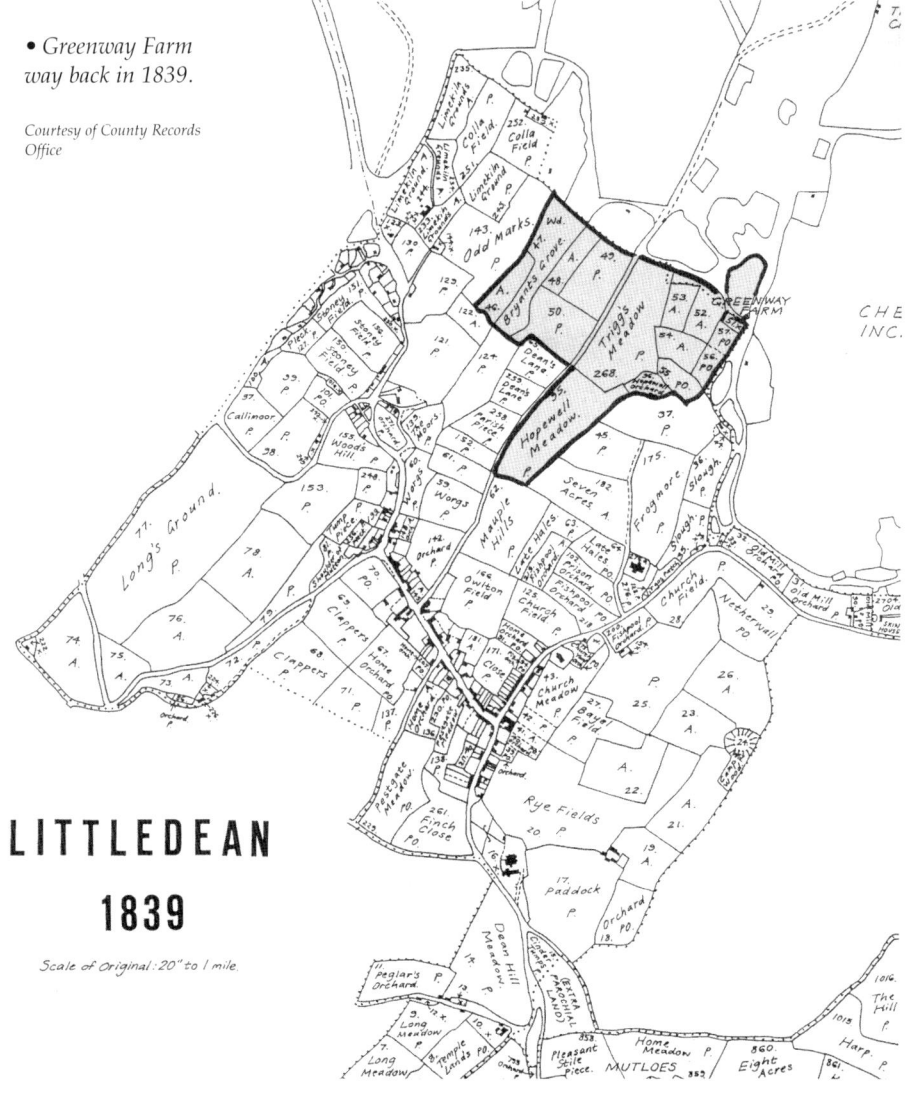

- *Greenway Farm way back in 1839.*

Courtesy of County Records Office

LITTLEDEAN

1839

Scale of Original: 20" to 1 mile.

Hopell and eventually Apple. And, by pure coincidence, there was a very old crab apple tree on the edge of the pond at one end of the pasture. The tree had been dead for a long time but still gave the appearance of being a thriving one because of a complete covering of dark green ivy. A pair of wood pigeons had seized upon it as a perfect nesting place and used it every year without fail. Below them, the twisted old tree-roots dangled into the edge of the nearby pond. It was fed by a small stream that flowed down over Fred Grindle's hilly farm, under the George Lane and then diagonally across our meat cleaver-shaped field.

The Big Meadow was in fact the same size as the Apple Meadow; both were exactly ten acres. There was no natural water source in the Big Meadow but there was a good barn, a fairly good slope for sledging and the whole pasture was, at different times of the year, covered in cowslips, buttercups and quite a few wild violets.

The Orchard had been cleared of most of the cider apple and pear trees a few years earlier, and now it provided a little extra grazing when the larger fields needed some time to recover. There were also a couple of smaller fields that were used for kale or beet crops and, finally, there was the Grove, the largest field of all. It was split into two very different parts. The Lower Grove was another ten acre grazing area that had originally been three tiny and separate fields; it had also been enlarged two years before by ploughing and cultivating as far up the rugged slope as was safe. A wire fence and gate now separated this from the Upper Grove, an area of some 17 acres of steep and very rough ground indeed. The gorse and brambles were doing their best to reclaim the area back to nature despite Father's annual effort to clear the worst of it. His attempt to remove the gorse by fire some years earlier still caused much mirth in the local pubs. Father had lost the plot and had succeeded in not just burning the gorse, but had also managed to reduce a hundred yard section of hedge to ashes!

There was a natural spring halfway up the slope. It was the source of a very small stream that trickled down between the anthills even in the middle of Summer. A large, stone horse-trough had somehow been dragged up there many years before and partly sunk into the ground. It ensured that there was a reservoir of cold, clear water for the animals all the year round. The play area was a wonderful wildlife sanctuary for kids but, other than that, it was rough grazing for our Scottish Black-face sheep and a spot of rabbiting now and then.

The farmhouse itself was an old, three storey building full of character, rodents and draughts. Huge oak beams were exposed in all the downstairs rooms as well as diagonal bracing timbers in the first and second floor bedrooms. They had all received many coats of black paint over the years and the ones which went from wall to floor were often the cause of a badly stubbed toe late at night. The top floor bedrooms, known affectionately as 'icebox canyon', were bitterly cold and the only natural light came from a small fanlight. There were some shivery Winter nights spent up there for sure. The rats had been cleared out of the house but a few persistent mice remained despite considerable efforts to remove them.

The outside of the house had been rendered to reduce the damp and then painted white. The surface gradually flaked away and, every few years or so, a new coat of 'Snocem' was added to maintain a tidy appearance. On one end of the house there was a long stone building; part of it was a large storage shed for coal and blocks, and the other part was a rather dilapidated affair which still housed a fully operational cider mill and press. Across the courtyard was a granary; the upstairs part was used for storage and the downstairs was home for a few hens and the boilers for the pig-swill.

In front of the elevated house and outbuildings was a half acre garden. Plum trees at the far end of it and along the one side all bore plenty of fruit in late Summer. An outside privy still stood proudly in one corner. In days gone by it must have been one hell of an effort to walk forty or so yards down steps and across an unlit garden on a dark, wet evening.

The soil in the garden was excellent for growing vegetables, although the side nearest the somewhat ineffective cesspit was left to fend for itself. Father dug the whole area by hand every year and grew enough potatoes and kidney beans to feed most of the village. There was the occasional setback however, like the time he tried to grow broad beans in a trench full of fresh pig's manure - it was not a great success.

My Father, Henry, was an ex Merchant Navy man. He had left school at an early age and had worked his way up through the ranks and had passed all his exams to become a Captain. Tragically for him, after surviving years of U-boat attacks in the North Atlantic, his hearing had deteriorated. It had been detected during a routine medical examination, but meant he could no longer continue in active service. He had become disillusioned; the sea had been his life since he was a lad and suddenly he had to become a landlubber. Farming was not his forte; his new civvy street job entailed travelling to work at RAF Records in Gloucester every day just to subsidise the farm; it did little towards making him any happier. He would tell aunt Kath and cousin Molly that when he was at sea he was the captain of the ship, but when at home he was just the knight of the broom!

The success of the farming venture was mainly due to Harold Beddis, the farm bailiff. With Harold came experience; not only was he a wizard with all animals, he was also a very good carpenter, builder and blacksmith. That array of skills resulted in us getting well constructed pigs cots, a second cowshed and a sheep dip - all built to last. Harold was also a lovely chap. He was small and wiry with a strange, overgrown crew-cut hairstyle. Maybe it was copied from the GI's, I'm not really sure, but by then he was in his mid 40's and it looked quite grey against his tanned complexion. He worked hard all day, every day, and never complained or saw any job as impossible. He once told me that the word 'can't' was not in his vocabulary. We would have fallen flat on our faces without his farming expertise and would have missed out on a lot of laughs as well.

I got home from school at the end of the first week feeling a bit more confident than I had been a few days earlier. I had discovered that some of the senior lads were really kind. Mike Bennett and Cliff Davies were typical of the nicer type of senior lad who would step in and stop any unnecessary bullying.

Meanwhile, my satchel was full of homework for the weekend. I shifted it onto my other shoulder as I paddled my new shoes in the straw and disinfectant bath just outside the gate. The recent foot and mouth outbreak had been very bad in the Forest area and had shocked the whole community. We had been incredibly lucky at Greenway. We had escaped any infection so far and there were hopes that the worst was over.

Harold was sat by Tony, my 17 year-old middle brother; they were enjoying a break before the evening milking session. They worked hard and well together and were the 'engine room' of the farming venture. Mother was the 'business brain' and, between them, they were making a success of the whole thing.

I negotiated my way around the discarded wellingtons in the porch and joined them at the table.

"It says in here", remarked Harold, nodding towards his copy of the *Mercury*, "that the parish council want a sign put up at Elton Corner".

"What do they want put on it?", asked Tony.

"The name of the capital of the Forest….Littledean!", replied Harold shaking his head, "…you'd think 'Bubbles' would have something better to do".

'Bubbles' was the affectionate nickname for Wilf Morris, the chairman of the parish council. He was an extremely friendly and helpful sort of chap.

"He has", interjected Mother, "we've had a letter from the council complaining about overhanging hedges in the George Lane".

"Jesus wept, we were planning to cut 'em next week", protested Harold, "we can't cut 'em in the middle of Summer you know".

"Good", said Mother, banging the teapot down on the table, "so you and Tony can make a start tomorrow then".

Mother was not very big, not much over five foot tall in fact, but when she banged a teapot it was no time to argue. Her cheeks went a little red and, with her jet black wavy hair, she reminded me of one of those little porcelain figurines.

Hedge cutting was not an easy job. Harold decided to start on the Big Meadow hedge as it was the worst. It was very overgrown; some of the blackthorn bushes were 12 feet tall or more. He grabbed two hedge-bills from the tractor shed, handed one to Tony, then started to whip the sharpening stone rapidly back and forward on the other. Soon it gleamed. He ran his thumb over the blade and, satisfied with the edge, handed the stone to Tony. By the time he returned with a quarter of a bale of straw, Tony had finished his sharpening and was busy loading stakes into the tractor box. They had accumulated several score of them during the previous months, ready for a hedge laying session. When the loading was all completed, Harold started up the little grey Ferguson.

Bob, our excitable Border Collie, barked his head off as usual, while Tony sat on the mudguard puffing his cigarette and contemplating the hard day ahead. He had learned to enjoy breaks as and when they occurred. At 17 years of age he was supremely fit, but he knew only too well that he had to pace himself or else Harold would work him to a standstill yet again.

The tractor stopped and Tony hopped off and opened the ancient five bar gate. Bob raced straight in hoping to find some sheep to chase. There were none; the meadow had not been grazed for a couple of weeks and the grass was starting to recover well. Lush, dark green circles of grass had sprung up around the cow-pats and there were a few mushrooms here and there. And, as they were close to the farmhouse, there was a fair chance of being able to collect enough for a decent meal before some of the bolder lads from the village turned up.

The tractor was parked in the corner of the Big Meadow next to the Pike House. The men surveyed the 300 yard section of hedge that ran along one side of the George Lane up as far as the edge of the Apple Meadow. Harold took a half-crown from his pocket.

"Heads or tails?"

"Heads", replied Tony.

"Hard luck....it's tails, you got the road side".

Tony grimaced; there was a three foot bank on the road side which made swinging a hedge-bill a lot harder. Then there was the traffic of course; every passing vehicle meant a mini tidy up and then squeezing into the hedge to let them pass.

The first stage was to clear out all the briers. Not a very nice job even with thick hedging gloves. They hacked and pulled until they had a twenty yard section relatively free of the more prickly stuff. Harold then used a bow-saw to thin out some of the small trees and Tony salvaged what he could to make more stakes. Then, armed with the hacker, Harold started to chop part way through some of the remaining blackthorn bushes. He made the cuts a foot or so off the ground then pushed each bush down into the hedge, taking care not to break them right off. Tony went on banging in stakes every couple of feet along the centre of the hedge. Harold then weaved the blackthorn in and out of the stakes to produce a 'living hurdle' effect. A final weave of nut-sticks on the top, together with a trim of the more bushier bits, and they had the beginning of a properly laid hedge.

The briers and blackthorn cuttings were piled up into a bonfire and, after checking the direction of the breeze, some straw pushed underneath with a pike. It took a few moments to catch properly and then it went up like an Australian bush fire. Flames engulfed the green leaves, as well as a couple of old blackbirds' nests, and sent a plume of blue smoke high into the air. Bits were landing all around them, many of them red hot.

"I think we had better have a fag", suggested Tony.

"Ay alright", replied Harold feeling they had made a damn good start and deserved one.

They lit up and squat down clear of the smoke and falling bits.

"Have you heard how Johnny Woodward is?", enquired Harold as he shifted his weight to the other knee.

" 'Im's going to be OK they reckon".

Johnny had come off his motorbike. He had been on his way home late at night on a lonely stretch of road from Blakeney. A sheep had run out into the road causing him to swerve violently. He lost control and was knocked unconscious. As time went on, his father had become more and more worried and eventually he and Mr Middlecote started a search. They soon found him in the middle of the road, still unconscious. He was of course rushed straight to hospital, where he eventually recovered and was none

• *Harold and Tony busy hedge laying along George Lane.*

the worse for the experience.

"That's good", said Harold, "we need him back in the team".

He was of course referring to Littledean Rovers, a team in which Tony was a more than useful player. Harold was the club secretary and marked out the pitch with a bag of sawdust every Saturday morning without fail.

Over the next couple of weeks the two men pressed on with the hedge laying, and I pressed on with school. We had been asked to sort ourselves out with woodwork aprons ready for a lesson later in the week. The job of making mine fell to Ruth Williams, an elderly blind lady who had come to live with us in the spare room. Ruth was a truly inspirational person. She was in her sixties by then, but had gone blind in her teens. She had been born and raised in St Ives in Cornwall and had emigrated to Canada where she had lost her sight, but never her joy of life. The sights and sounds of her childhood were as clear as if she could see them. In fact she still could, captured in her mind for all time. I had been amazed before with how she could knit pullovers of complex design for me without any reliance on a pattern. It therefore came as no surprise when she set about making the apron. With Mother's reluctance to spend money, neither was it much of a surprise when I saw that the raw materials were an old cow-cake sack and some white ribbon material.

The finished apron was very good. Ruth had somehow transformed the sack into something I was quite proud of. By then I was really looking forward to the double woodwork lesson. When the day finally arrived, all the girls headed off to the Domestic Science room; the boys made their way to Mr Fern's little workshop area next to the canteen at the end of the girls' yard. The atmosphere was a little more relaxed than normal lessons and we were eager to make a start.

Mr Fern was short and well rounded. He seemed to be middle-aged, although it was hard to tell with those chubby red cheeks and tight, curly black hair with the odd bit of silver showing through. He stood before us wearing a dark grey apron.

"Can all you boys see this?" asked Mr Fern, pointing to a length of half inch wooden doweling-rod resting on two hooks high on the wall.

There was a general mumbling of agreement from the class.

"This is Archibald", he continued, "and if you step out of line with me then you will get to know him very well indeed".

We were to find out in due course how prophetic those words were in that first lesson.

"Right then boys, now that you have met Archibald you can put on your aprons and we'll make a start".

I donned my sack-bag, managed to tie a bow behind my back, and then looked around. There were black aprons, grey ones, white ones and all different shapes and sizes. My eyes came to rest on Ray Roberts. Ray came from Cinderford and lived close to another classmate, John Young. All three of us belonged to the small and nippy brigade and we got on well together. However, I soon realised that no-one at all was looking at me and my sack-bag, the whole class was transfixed with Ray. It wasn't his apron that got everyone's attention, it was what was on it. Someone started sniggering and then we all joined in.

"Stop that you boys.....what is going on?"

"Please sir it's Roberts' apron sir", replied Frankie Beech, the boy who happened to be in line with Mr Fern's gaze.

"Well what's funny about that....?"

He pointed at Ray's chest where he was self conscientiously covering the top of his apron with his hands.

"Move your hands boy".

Ray's hands moved slowly away and revealed a beautifully embroidered bunch of flowers.

"What on earth is that – boy?"

"Please sir my mum thought it would look nicer with some flowers on it".

We laughed until the tears ran down our cheeks. Ray was known as 'Flowery' from that day forth!

Chapter Two
Autumn 1956

The boys in my class were all instructed to go to Room 6 - Mr Butcher's form room. Luckily Mr Butcher only taught maths to the senior pupils. I say luckily because he did seem to be a rather stern, no nonsense type to me. There were not going to be many laughs in his classes, I was quite sure of that. We were lined up in front of a wardrobe in the corner of the room. Mr Butcher opened the door to reveal a small mountain of school caps.

One by one we were hauled over and a cap thrust down onto our heads. Years of experience of fitting caps, or at least making caps fit, meant a very quick, if rough fitting. We were also given a small shield-shaped enamel badge which had to be sewn on the front of the red, blue and yellow caps.

Mother duly sewed on the badge that same evening while I packed my brand new rugby shirt, 'nicks' and boots ready for a double games period the following afternoon. I slept soundly, looking forward to our first sports session.

The next morning was crisp and bright although there was no real warmth in the early sun. The very first of the leaves were beginning to turn yellow and there was a heavy dew on the grass. Spiders had worked furiously all night long, their webs were everywhere, all covered in a fine coating of moisture which made them stand out so clearly. I knocked a couple off the gate by accident as I opened it, and felt sorry for the destruction of their painstaking work.

I pulled my new cap down firmly onto my head, adjusted my dangling rugby boots, and set off along the George Lane. It was a good-to-be-alive day I thought to myself as I stepped out smartly and full of optimism. The bus arrived on time and a group of us chattered as we eventually made our way down Station Street to school. It all seemed so normal now and even the morning lessons flew by.

All the first year boys joined in the same games session. Typically there would be around forty of us. We were expected to make our own way on foot from Station Street at the bottom of Cinderford, right the way up to Virgo's farm on the top of the hill overlooking Ruspidge. It was the best part of two miles, all of it uphill.

I walked steadily up towards the Picture House with Royston Wellington and David Holder. Royston was my good friend from Littledean Primary school days, but David was a new pal. Fresh faced, freckled and under a mop of curly brown hair, he lived in Cinderford just a few hundred yards from our school. We probably hit it off because he was a complete toe-rag as well. What we had not calculated however, was that Double View Secondary school lunch-break was at the same time as our trek. Shouting 'Double View blockheads' out of the bus window earlier had perhaps not been such a good idea after all.

There we were with our brand new caps and laden down with satchels and rugby kit.

"Well look what we've got here", sneered one of the older boys.

He snatched Royston's cap and threw it to one of his mates. After some jostling and pushing, mine and David's cap were taken as well. They passed them around rugby style for a bit then decided to play football. The dirt and dust covered things were finally slung over a garden wall next to the library.

"I'll tell my mam of you", sobbed Royston.

"A fat lot of good that'll do you", I thought to myself.

We recovered our caps and dusted them down as best we could. Luckily the badges were still intact.

"I 'ent wearing a cap up here again", vowed David, "and what's more we'll go along Church Street in future".

There were no arguments to that suggestion. We negotiated Belle Vue road without further attack and turned across to Mount Pleasant. There we crossed the road and climbed a stile into Mr Virgo's farm. A made-up track meandered its way across several fields until, in the middle of absolutely no-where, we reached the games field. There were a couple of little wooden cricket pavilions in two of the corners, one for boys and one for girls; these were the changing rooms. There was only a sink and tap, so if you got really plastered in mud, then that was more or less how you remained until you got home.

The games master was Mr Geoff Goddard, a small hatchet-faced man who reminded me of a whippet. He was more than willing to dole out corporal punishment, always a 'dap' applied viciously and repeatedly to your rear end. He had his favourites, not surprisingly it was the ones who were particularly good and keen at sport. Toe-rags were not to be tolerated. David Holder, myself and a few of our other mates were in for a rough time.

The next hour was spent on ball handling and tackling. Towards the end of the session, Mr Goddard decided to practice a full scrum.

"Haines....you can be hooker, ...Mayo and Hendy second row.....".

He reeled off the names of both packs and assembled us in a crouching position. We were made to engage slowly. It is hard to describe the agony of being compressed from all sides for the first time. I thought both shoulders were dislocated and my backside was heaved up between my ears.

"Who would ever be a hooker?...."

My legs were almost paralysed by the time Mr Goddard finally lobbed the ball into the scrum.

"Hook it now", he shouted.

I could only think of a hospital bed. Eventually, after what seemed like hours, we were allowed to disengage. I straightened up and checked for any breakage.

"OK Lewis....you swap with Haines".

Colin Lewis was put in as hooker and I was put in the centre.

"There is a God up there", I thought.

- *Roy Barton leads the race up on the sports field on Virgo's Farm , near Mount Pleasant.*

Photo courtesy of Roy Mills

I walked home after games still wearing my rugby kit and with my school clothes screwed up in a bag. It was an easy walk along the top of Littledean Hill. The tree-ringed Roman Camp was way below to my right, and beyond that through the haze I could see part of the Horseshoe Bend of the Severn. I paused at the little shop near the Foresters pub. It belonged to John Young's aunt Bessie. But, unable to rustle up enough money for some chocolate, I headed reluctantly on down past Fred Grindle's house and onto Jack Hayward's farm. I sat on a stile at the top of the Grove and could see Tony way below me. He was walking across to Apple Meadow to move the electric fence. We were strip grazing to make the most of the good grass. It took me the best part of five minutes to reach him.

"What happened...did Alfie Hinds get you?" he remarked, looking down his nose at my dishevelled appearance

Tony was referring to an escaped prisoner who had been on the run for some time, and had supposedly been sighted in virtually every county by then. Before I could reply, a rabbit hopped slowly by. Something was wrong with it, you could tell straightaway. It kept stopping and didn't seem to know where it was going. The poor creature ran blindly into the small stream that ran down the middle of the field. It then scrambled back out somehow and came back towards me. I could then see that its eyes were swollen right up and closed completely.

"Tony....what's wrong with this rabbit?"

He walked back to me and took one look.

"It has got that myxy".

Tony was referring to myxomatosis which had been spreading like wildfire in the area, but that was my first close up view of it. It was truly horrible. He walked back, picked up a metal electric fence pole and returned. The rabbit was motionless, wet and bedraggled. Tony dispatched it with a single, hard blow. It was a merciful thing to do. I wondered how many hundreds of creatures were suffering like that poor thing. It was a cruel disease. I never ate rabbit ever again.

Later we were sat around the table. Father and Tony on one side and me on the other.

"With all this trouble in Egypt I wonder if our Dave will get called up", said Mother as she placed a plate of sandwiches in front of us…....

Dave was my eldest brother; he was 24 now and married to Pat. They and their young baby, Sue, lived halfway up the Plump Hill in Mitcheldean. He had fought with the Glosters just over five years earlier and had suffered badly as a POW. Roy Mills from Cinderford was one of a number of brave young local lads who fought at the Imjin River battle and were then taken prisoner. Roy gave me his account of how Dave fell foul of the Chinese:

'We were on a timber cutting and hauling detail at the Yalu river camp. They worked us hard and also worked the oxen and mules until they dropped. They then were killed and eaten. We had a Chinese cook at the time who was not right in the head. He had a habit of eating the raw eyes of the dead animals. The prisoners would egg him on to eat some more, and he would oblige by scrunching them up with a loopy grin on his face.

'One day we returned from working and saw the cook hacking away at the throat of an ox with a carving knife. Dave didn't care about much, but he did not like to see cruelty to animals. He picked up a large sledge hammer and motioned the cook out of the way. One mighty blow between the eyes and the ox fell pole-axed to the ground. The animal was then stuck and put out of its agony. As a result of this the Chinese gave Dave the slaughtering job from then on.

'It all worked well for a short while. He stole small pieces of meat to supplement the awful food and to facilitate escape attempts. Roy was one of a number who helped Dave and the rest of the escape committee. But then Dave got caught; for him the following eight months were very bad indeed....'

"I shouldn't think so", replied Father, "by the time they get round to calling him up it'll all be over".

Mother nodded her head hoping that he was right, she didn't ever again want to face the awful waiting for news that she had experienced back in 1951.

Just then Harold poked his head around the door.

"Have you heard about Tom Rogers?"

"No", replied Father.

"Well 'im's in hospital".

Tom was 'Podgy' Rogers' father. 'Podgy' was a chum from my Littledean Primary days. They lived in the Folders estate, next door to Bernard Giles and not far from the George Hotel. It seemed that Tom had slipped on the icy road outside his house and knocked himself out. He was taken to Gloucester Hospital and stitched up.

"Had he been taking any refreshment?", enquired Father.

"It's possible", said Harold smiling broadly, "see you all tomorrow".

The following afternoon, Martha, one of our sows, started to chew up the straw in her cot. It was a sure sign that she would farrow during the night. I don't know why most of our sows seemed to farrow in the middle of the night, but they did. Harold watched her lie down, stand back up, chew some more straw then repeat it all over again. It was always down to him to oversee the farrowing as he was the best skilled to deal with any complications.

There was a heating lamp installed in the covered part of the cot; it was designed to provide warmth to new-born piglets on such sharp Autumn nights. Martha finally settled herself down with her back against the farrowing rail. This was like a very low handrail, positioned about a foot off the ground and a foot from the wall. It was to prevent a careless mother from lying down and crushing her youngsters against the wall; the rail always gave them a little escape route.

At dusk, Harold took an old milking stool into the cot, switched on the lamp, lit up a Players Navy Cut and made himself comfortable. The part stone, part brick little building seemed warm and cosy in the glowing light and surrounded by straw. He spoke softly to Martha who did not stir. She was breathing heavily, her complete side was rising and falling with each lung-full of air.

"Won't be long now", he thought.

Harold was right. Within minutes the first piglet popped out. He picked it up, wiped it all over with straw until it was clean and white, and then placed it against its mother's teat. I was always amazed how much a new-born piglet looked like a puppy. At that early age, the ears flopped down and the nose was stumpy; it looked nothing at all like the snout on a grown up sow.

Over the next hour Martha had seven more young ones; all were healthy and suckling well. However, Harold knew from bitter experience that the time between the first and last piglet could be hours. He lit up another cigarette and listened to the sounds of the night. He heard foxes screaming up on the top of the Grove, an owl hooting somewhere across the Common and the roof timbers creaking and groaning. Martha's breathing was still heavy, but that was her third litter and she was well in control.

It must have been an hour later when the ninth and last piglet was born. Harold wiped it down and cleared up. When he was satisfied that all nine were warm and settled, he slowly walked back to the Land Rover. It seemed to make an almighty racket as it started up and, as it was the middle of the night, he almost tip-toed it down to the George Lane and off home.

It was Saturday the next day and, when Royston Wellington called to go 'conkering', I showed him the litter.

"They look like dogs", he remarked.

I was really pleased that at last someone else had finally made the same observation as me.

We set off down the bumpy old track leading to the Pike House. Both of us picked up some stones and had a bit of throwing practice, firstly at the Big Meadow gatepost and then at the corrugated roof of the nearby barn. The stones pinged off the roof leaving small shiny dents on the rusty panels. Our arms soon ached from the effort and so we strolled on along George Lane. Royston looked closely at the newly laid Big Meadow hedge.

"Won't be many nests in there next time", he observed.

He was right; the severely cropped hawthorn was less than four feet high and densely weaved with no more small trees and bushes for chaffinches and dunnocks. There were plenty of other unkempt hedges however, and the birds were never really going to be short of nesting sites on the farm.

• *Watched by the owl in Apple Meadow Barn.*

We mooched on towards Littledean, stopping eventually for a rest against the Apple Meadow gate. A barn owl was perched in the loft doorway of the partly crumbling barn. It was often there and looked across at us with a mixture of suspicion and disdain. The nearby pond was very full so we gathered up as many stones as we could and lobbed then aimlessly into the water. The commotion must have disturbed the owl as, when we headed on up the road, it had taken its leave.

We cut up through the Folders Estate. Ronny Giles was by his backdoor busily removing the previous week's mud from his football boots ready for a match in the afternoon. Sat on the pavement opposite were Bernard Giles, 'Podgy' Rogers and Fred Niblett.

"Where are you off to?" asked 'Podgy'.

"Nowhere....just got to get some stuff from the shop", I replied vaguely.

I wasn't telling them we were going 'conkering' or else they would get to know about our secret tree; besides there wouldn't be many each if we shared out five ways. We kept walking and were soon on the little path leading down to the Co-op. Some girls were talking down by the phone box; when we got nearer I could see that it was Jean Hodges and Dorothy Hart. They were saying something to Dorothy Phelps on the other side of the road. It was probably a witches curse; all those three needed was a few toads and a cauldron and they would have been well away! There was a sort of embarrassed 'hello' between us; boys didn't talk to girls very much.

Inside the Co-op I could see Harold's brother, Cedric. He was wearing his usual clean white smock. He had worked in the shop for as long as I could remember. We pressed on down the road and managed to get as far as the King's Head without further unwanted questions. By the time we turned up Silver Street we felt quite safe that we were not being followed.

• *The magnificent Dean Hall.* Photo courtesy of Cinderford Library

At the elbow of the street we passed the house belonging to Mr and Mrs Bullock. They had been very unlucky some years earlier when a runaway truck had hit their house. The truck was really an old ambulance with the top and part of the sides cut off it. It belonged to Harold and was a bit of a wreck. It had to be bump started every morning and so Harold parked it at the top of the field which sloped down to the back of his house and the rest of Silver Street. He was called out in the early hours one morning to find his truck buried in the back of the Bullock's house. A chimney and part of the back wall was partly dismantled and Harold's beloved vehicle was a complete write off. What the police found so amazing was how the vehicle had free-wheeled 200 yards down the slope and had somehow missed dozens of trees on the way down. Harold reckoned it had been kids messing about and that they had jumped clear and let it go. It wasn't much consolation to Mr and Mrs Bullock!

However, our destination was the giant conker tree up at Pleasant Stile, almost directly opposite to Dean Hall. That historical building was reckoned to go back to Roman times, in fact there was the site of a Temple nearby with a water shrine believed to be to Sabrina, the Goddess of the river; she certainly would have enjoyed a magnificent view out over the Severn Horseshoe.

Our immediate objective was less historic however, it was in Mr Wellington's field, just a few feet away and over the other side of a stone wall. 'Sunny Butty' was how most people referred to Mr Wellington. He was a pleasant but eccentric chap who was no relation to Royston. He generally wore a squashed Trilby hat, a long Mac and leather gaiters, and peered out through a pair of thick lens spectacles. His smallholding was the home to a motley mixture of sheep, pigs and hens. It was fortunate that neither Dave nor Tony had yet been caught on their regular egg raids on 'Sunny Butty's' coop!

There was no sign of him that day so we both hopped up onto the wall; it was only a few feet high and there were plenty of footholds. It was possible to reach a few spiky burrs from tiptoe on the wall, but there were already plenty of others down on the ground over in the field.

"Let's put 'em in a pile and divide 'em afterwards", suggested Royston.

It was a good suggestion; it saved racing to open only the most promising burrs and squabbling over them. Beside, splitting up the pile would be done by alternately selecting one at a time. It was much fairer, we used the same process for picking football teams down on the Recreation Ground, although nobody wanted to be last choice – the hopeless one!

We spent the next quarter of an hour throwing sticks up at the tree, just trying to dislodge some of the more healthy looking conkers from the higher branches. When we were tired of that, we stopped and carefully broke open all the burrs to reveal the beautiful, rich-red and white conkers inside. There were some real beauties, both in size and shape. I pointed at Royston and commenced the age-old rhyme to decide who was to go first….

"Ibble obble black bobble
ibble obble out,
turn a dirty dishcloth inside out;
so out you must go
'cos I said so"

- *A game of conkers at school.*

If the cap fits

It helped of course to know when using the rhyme with only two people, that whoever you pointed to at the start was also going to be pointed to at the end. I never did burden Royston with that additional information.

The dividing up process was slow to begin with. There was some painstaking checking and rechecking over the first three or four selections. They were the very best conkers, the ones with championship potential. We must have ended up with thirty or so each and maybe ten were really big and round like a golf-ball. We would never have thought of bringing some bags to put them in, and so we ended up with every pocket stuffed right full.

Getting back over the wall wasn't as easy as earlier; the bulging pockets saw to that. Once we were back on the road we did our best to look nonchalant. We ambled back down Silver Street and decided to go down past the Church rather than the Folders route; it was much quieter and we were less likely to give away the location of our secret conker tree. Ray Cage and his younger brother Norman watched us go by with a suspicious 'what-are-you-doing-here' look. Just then their father called them from inside the house and they went back in at some speed.

"Do you remember Mr Meek having a go at me for saying 'bust'?", said Royston as we passed the Primary school.

I nodded, remembering that Wilf Meek had not been in a good mood that day. He had asked Royston why railway tracks had small gaps left in them. In fairness Royston had given a correct answer. He had said it was to allow for expansion or else the tracks would bust.

"They will what?", yelled Mr Meek.

Flustered, Royston thought he was totally wrong with his answer.

"They will what?", repeated Mr Meek, even more loudly.

By then half the kids in the class were whispering 'burst.....burst..', but Royston was in blind panic by then, he just couldn't hear anything or anybody; his eyes were fixed on the incandescent Mr Meek who looked as if he was about to burst a blood vessel himself.

The torture went on for several minutes before Fred Niblett whispered 'burst' so loud that Mr Meek thought Royston had finally got the correct answer. Oh happy days, except for poor Royston that was.

We pressed on down to the Gaol and took the track across Henry Boughton's fields. The grass was nice and dry by and so our lightweight daps were fine. A few minutes later we reached the sanctuary our own Big Meadow. Over on our right were some foxholes that had been dug among the roots of the hedge and a lone oak tree nearby. Large mounds of red earth were piled up in front of the dens indicating recent activity. The distinctive earthy smell of fox was all around; I thought to myself that the poultry had better be securely penned from then on.

It was lunch-time when we finally got back to the farm. Royston was under strict orders from his father to be back home on time. His father was a scowling, grumpy man and his cauliflower ears indicated an earlier interest in pugilism; it was best that Royston got back for lunch per instructions.

There were all sorts of theories of how best to produce a champion conker; some liked to soak them in vinegar, others liked to part bake them and so on. Royston reckoned to leave them in the fire hearth for a few days, but I preferred to leave them as they were , untreated. I thought shrinking the inner flesh to make the outer skin hard was not a wise move and liked a conker to be heavy and leathery. I got a small meat skewer from the kitchen and disappeared into the tractor shed, well away from prying eyes.

The best of my conkers was a spherical one about the size of a golf-ball. Its shape would deflect blows much better than the flatter ones. I carefully inserted the skewer into the centre of the white patch on the one side and, with minimal pressure, started twisting gently to and fro. It was vital not to break through the other side and leave splits around the hole. I stopped several times and blew the loose bits. Eventually a tiny bump appeared on the bottom of the conker - the skewer was almost through. A few more gentle twists and the job was complete; a small clean hole with no splits. Then came a touch of professionalism; I tied a large knot on the end of a length of string, making sure it was much bigger that the hole. I then hunted out a small washer and threaded it onto the string followed by the conker. My theory was that the washer prevented the knot being forced into the conker and possibly cracking it. It had worked before, all I could do then was to try it out.

I just couldn't wait for Monday morning; it wasn't the Latin with Mr Aveston or double French with Miss Birde-Jones that excited me, it was to throw out a challenge to all 'conkerers'. In the morning break I won two matches so mine was then a conker number two. It was a good start and at lunch-time I won another.

A second year boy swaggered over.

"Want a game?", he asked, swinging what looked like a tennis ball on a piece of baling string.

"What conker is yours?"

"Seven", he replied, looking over his shoulder at some mates.

I wasn't sure whether or not to believe him, but could hardly refuse the challenge anyway.

"Obbly obbly onker my first conker", he added quickly.

"Damn it", I thought, "he's got first knock". I just wasn't on the ball.

We found a quiet place down by the bike sheds where prefects and nosey-parkers couldn't see us. John Young and Royston were my Seconds. It was his first go. I wrapped my string around my knuckles several times and left a good length down to the conker. It was imperative that a good grip was maintained because if it flew out of your hand then you'd had it.

He got in a decent first knock but caused no damage. I shortened my string by wrapping it around my first two fingers a couple of times and then pulled it tight by holding my conker in my left hand. We exchanged knocks for several rounds without any visible damage, but then I did get in a cracker of a knock and started a small split on his number seven. He panicked a bit and all but missed on his next go. I then caught him another beauty and somehow his string twisted around mine and got wrenched from his grip. Number seven crashed onto the tarmac and disintegrated.

The second year lad looked down in disbelief at his beloved conker. I was ecstatic and started a victory celebration. Just then the bell sounded and saved me from any further repercussions.

Lightly Poached

Chapter Three
Late 1956

Harold was in the tractor shed. It was a small, lean-to building tacked onto the side of the main barn as an afterthought. Violet, our huge Chestnut mare, had been retired for some time and now the Ferguson needed a dry roof over it on wet and wintry days. The workbench inside was cluttered with tools; there was a pig-net hanging from one beam, cross-cut saws from another and all sorts of harness dangling from six inch nails driven into the wall. The pig-net hadn't been used for ages and a wren had built its domed nest in it a couple of years earlier. And, although it had gone brown and dusty, it was still in perfect condition.

He was pumping up a football. Beads of sweat were starting to appear as a result of the furious elbow movement. Having a cigarette parked in his mouth was not making the operation any easier, but if he put it down then he was sure to forget all about it; a risky thing to do with nearly forty tons of precious hay on the other side of some slit windows.

He squeezed the ball then bounced it a couple of times to test the pressure. When satisfied, he pushed the valve in and started to do up the lace. The real skill was to tuck the ends in so they didn't come out during the match. Many an eyebrow had been split open when heading a heavy ball with a dangling lace.

As secretary and general workhorse for Littledean Rovers, Harold's duties seemed extensive. They ranged from cutting the hedge around the pitch to putting up nets, marking out and dealing with anything else that cropped up. On fine days I liked to help, particularly with the marking out. A large sack-bag, filled to the brim with sawdust, was the key requirement for that. There were no machines to put down nice straight white lines, only handfuls of sawdust placed every yard or so. On wet, muddy days, the referee and linesmen had a devil of a job spotting where the line had been prior to the sliding tackles that had by then obliterated it.

We often recalled a game that had taken place some three years earlier; the Reserves had been scheduled to take on Staunton in the afternoon and Tony was expecting a hard game. It turned out to be a very hard and painful game indeed for Keith James. During

• *The wren's nest in the tractor shed.*

one spell of play, the ball went loose and two Rovers players tried to clear it at the same time. Chippy Walding lashed at the ball, missed it completely and managed to kick his own team-mate. Keith went down in agony with a badly broken leg.

I am not sure what Harold's background was in first aid, but he straightened out Keith's legs, got him comfortable and applied splints. Bernard Giles, 'Podgy' Rogers and I stood close by, staring at Keith's distorted face. Harold then took the belt off his tattered old raincoat and carefully tied it around both legs.

Someone had run to call for an ambulance from the phone-box up in the village, but it seemed like an eternity before it eventually drove through the gate and across the pitch. We watched in fearful silence as Keith was lifted up into the back. Wilf James hopped up in as well and accompanied the poor lad to the hospital.

Keith's brother, Roy, normally played for the first team, however they didn't have a game that particular Saturday. He strolled down through the village just after tea-time.

"How's thy Keith doing?", enquired Jim Giles.

"What are you on about?", replied Roy, quite oblivious to the drama of the previous hour.

"'Bust his leg....or at least had it bust for 'im, and Wilf James went into hospital with 'im".

Roy's plans for a stop at the George were shattered. He raced home to tell his father and somehow they got themselves organised and into the hospital.

Poor Keith was in plaster for 18 weeks. It was at the same time that Bill Kibble broke his leg playing for Popes Hill. The locals got together and organised a charity football match to raise funds for the two boys. They got £26 each; a significant amount of money in those days, especially for Keith, because he had lost his job as well.

It was some time later that Keith was called up to do his National Service; he was in fact about to be posted to Germany when his father was taken seriously ill. When there was little more that could be done for him, he was discharged from hospital and sent home. Roy was the eldest of the children and, as their mother had died some time earlier, it fell to him to somehow get Keith back home to see his father for the last time.

Roy went down to Cinderford Police Station and explained the situation to them. They readily agreed that if Keith's C.O. phoned the Station they would verify the events and support the case for compassionate leave.

The next step was to somehow contact Keith who was in or near to Folkestone. Roy knew that he had arranged to phone his girlfriend Pearl before he sailed. He reasoned that if he could get a message to the C.O. via Keith, then the C.O. could phone the Police and let him come home.

Roy managed to get a lift up to Ruardean Woodside with Idris Teague, an old family friend. They spotted Pearl in the phone-box just below the Roebuck Inn. She was obviously still waiting for the call and so they knew they were in time. They parked nearby; Roy then ripped open the phone-box door to a terrified Pearl who thought she was being attacked. When she had calmed down, he explained what it was all about.

They all waited for another half an hour or more but no call came.

"I'll bet that so-and-so got on the boat and totally forgot to ring", said Pearl dejectedly.

They reluctantly agreed to call it a day, bitterly disappointed that their one hope of contacting Keith hadn't worked out. Idris got back into the car and slammed the door. At that moment the phone started ringing.

"You answer or he might ring off if he hears a man's voice", whispered Roy.

It was Keith on the phone; he wasn't a so-and-so after all! Pearl explained that Roy needed to speak to him urgently. Roy then told him of his father's desperately serious condition and asked him to get his C.O. to phone Cinderford Police straightaway.

The compassionate leave was granted and Keith caught the next train up to Paddington and on to Gloucester. He arrived there at around 4.30am; there was no-one around and it didn't occur to him to try and phone for a taxi. He started walking home, still in full uniform, and had reached Highnam Corner before he spotted a milk-van. Waving his arms frantically, he managed to flag him down and get a lift as far as Longhope. The march up to the top of the Plump Hill made the sweat run out of him but he pushed himself to keep going.

Keith reached his garden gate at breakfast time; Roy met him there to tell him that sadly his father had died only minutes earlier.

The army were very helpful, Keith was not sent abroad and eventually he got posted to Robinswood barracks just outside Gloucester. From there he cycled home to Littledean Hill as often as he could to check that the rest of the family were OK. The exercise certainly verified that his broken leg had mended properly, that was for sure!

All that had been recent history; in the meantime, Harold and I had to finish putting out the sawdust ready for the match that afternoon. Littledean Rovers were entertaining RAF Innsworth.

I was there later in the afternoon watching together with a handful of other die-hard spectators. It started to rain not long after the kick-off but there just wasn't anywhere to shelter. I could overhear Jim Giles talking to Harold who was trying to run the line at the same time.

"Have you heard about Danny Beard?", asked Jim.

"No". Harold shook his head and kept his eyes focused on the ball.

"Not heard about the cheques then?"

At that point there was a surging attack by Innsworth and Harold raced to keep up. He was slow off the mark and 20 yards behind the play but waved his now sodden white handkerchief to indicate offside. It was a controversial decision and the forwards were incensed. Their actual comments referred to needing an eye test and sticking his handkerchief where it shouldn't be kept really. The language used was a lot more direct and colourful though.

Harold shuffled back along the line, eventually to within hearing distance of Jim Giles.

"Ay....this bloke from Cinderford called into Danny's shop apparently and asked him if he would cash a cheque for £2 10s. Well...as he knew this bloke by sight, he took the cheque and handed over the money. He....."

Harold charged off again, determined that time to keep up with play. It was not easy; he was wearing wellingtons and an old mac; explosive bursts of speed were no longer that easy. His greying crew-cut was gradually flattening out from all the rain and the shoulders of his mac were absolutely saturated. It was hard work and his every decision was now the subject of an argument.

Again, the Rovers saw off the attack and Harold inched his way back towards the halfway line.

"Well this blokey disappeared with the readies but returned later and asked Danny if he could cash another cheque, this time for 30 bob".

"What was the problem then?", asked Harold.

"The problem was that the bloke didn't have his cheque book with him the second time".

"Oh...I see".

"Well you know that Danny is the trusting sort and he handed over the 30 bob".

"What happened then?"

By now Harold had got interested in the story and his attention to the game had wandered.

"Absolutely nothing......the bloke beggared off and didn't come back....Danny had to call the Police", said Jim slapping his thigh and laughing at the shopkeeper's misfortune.

Suddenly there was a shrill blast on the whistle. Harold looked around and saw that the ball was in the net and the Innsworth forwards were jogging back with arms raised in triumph. The Rovers defenders, Tony among them, looked at Harold in disbelief.

"The bloody number nine was at least five yards offside", raged Tony.

Harold kept his handkerchief, and his eyes, well down. Mercifully there was an equaliser late on, so at least a defeat was avoided. There wasn't a lot of discussion about it over the rest of the weekend; on the farm Harold was the foreman after all and Tony was just the worker.

Monday morning came around all too quickly and it was time for school again. I packed a pair of black 'daps' and some shorts ready for a P.E. lesson later in the morning. The trip to school was uneventful and, for once, I didn't have to worry about cribbing any homework as I had managed to do it all for a change.

Just outside Tim's office was a huge mountain of coke. Mr Verry, the caretaker, was shovelling away at it to replenish the boilers. He was a quiet, serious sort of chap, but it was woe betide any boy who climbed up onto the coke pile and spread it all over the yard.

We had Mr Goddard's delightful company to look forward to after the first break. In fact P.E. could be one of two extremes - either highly enjoyable or downright awful. The enjoyable part was playing a game of 'pirates' for example; in that game, all shapes and sizes of equipment were arranged around the gym and a sort of off-ground-tag was played, whereby if you touched the ground or were tagged, then you were out. It was great fun, wonderful exercise and we enjoyed it thoroughly. The awful part was being made to do things your body didn't want to; one of these was the 'crab'.

To do the crab you first had to lie on your back. You then raised your knees and put the soles of your feet flat on the ground. Finally, with your elbows pointing upwards, you put your palms on the ground behind your shoulders, with the fingers pointing towards your feet. You then heaved yourself upwards into a 'C' shape and, looking like a distorted stick insect, you were expected to walk around.

The linesman's error

I glanced under my armpit and across to John Young and 'Flowery' Roberts; it was not a pretty sight and it gave me a fair idea of how hideous I must have looked without a shirt on. Some of the heftier lads like Richard Holland and Bill Edginton were excused that torture. Lucky them!

The following weekend I arranged to go 'chestnutting' with David Holder. He had cycled down from Cinderford a couple of times before and enjoyed the rough and tumble of life on the farm. He was due down around mid-morning, but first I had to help cleaning out the cowsheds.

It wasn't really hard work, it was just messy and repetitive. Firstly, using a long-handled brush, all the muck was swept into the central gutter and shovelled into a barrow. This was then struggled around to the dung-heap some forty yards away and finally, the concrete was washed down with cold water and scrubbed thoroughly with the hard brush. Both cowsheds had cold water supplies and so, apart from the possibility spilling the water down inside your Wellingtons, it wasn't too bad.

"You want to be careful where you spill that mind", said Harold with his forefinger in the air.

"I 'ent trying to get wet feet on purpose Harold".

"I 'ent on about that old butt, just keep the water away from them 'electrics'; some chap up at Worcester managed to electrocute 11 cows by splashing water onto faulty wiring".

He nodded towards some power points; it sounded really serious so I took special care as I finished off. Just then David Holder popped his head around the cowshed door.

"Hiya....you ready?"

"Yep.....coming now".

I quickly changed out of my wellingtons and into some old brown lace-up shoes. We headed across the Green and on towards 'Long 'un' Brain's house which was situated in a beautiful but lonely spot on the edge of the Chestnuts Wood Inclosure. It was a spot not far from where the Italian POW's had worked on timber hauling just over a decade earlier.

A brown and black dog ran up and down 'Long 'un's' garden fence, barking furiously as he did so.

"Does it bite?" asked David.

"Only if it can catch you", I replied with a smirk, safe in the knowledge that the garden gate was always kept closed.

We edged on by and continued in the general direction of Welshbury Wood. The barking behind us had gradually tailed off by the time we disturbed a sizeable flock of Welsh tats that had been grazing in a clearing. There were always some lush, green patches in those clearings and verges, and one sheep badger or another would dump his animals in the wood to take advantage of the free food.

They crashed through the fallen leaves and dying fern making the noise of a herd of elephants as they did so. They kept going until they were a good hundred yards away before stopping and looking back indignantly at the assumed threat.

There were plenty of chestnuts on the ground and squirrels were grabbing what they could for the Winter ahead. We had already seen three or four of them but we were not on a shooting expedition. David built up a pile of spiky shells and I scuffed them open with the sole of my shoe. Within half an hour we had filled every pocket and were having to put the rest down inside our shirts.

Except for our fingers, which looked like pincushions and felt as tender as hell, it had been a very successful expedition. And, because it was still quite early, we decided to press on to Welshbury Wood, peeling and eating nuts as we went.

"Is there a bull in there?", asked David, not yet confident with all farm animals.

"No", I replied in a dismissive sort of way, "just a few sheep...that's all".

We got over the creaky old stile into the field that stood between us and Fowlhead barn on the very edge of the wood.

"Watch out", I yelled at the top of my voice.

David was gone in a flash. He never ran like that for Geoff Goddard I can tell you. He was inside the barn before my echo had stopped.

"You silly beggar", he said sheepishly as he came back out.

We laughed our heads off as we made our way up the winding path leading to the high point of the wood. A number of the small trees had shed most of their leaves and now revealed several old jay and pigeon nests.

"We'll come here next year and get some eggs", said David eyeing up the trees for climbing difficulty.

"Good idea", I replied, glad that our friendship had long-term possibilities after the earlier prank.

A few minutes later we reached the huge beech tree whose roots seemed to bind together the mound which formed the top of the hill. The whole area was rumoured to have been a Roman Camp similar to the one just east of Littledean, and some kids reckoned they had found arrowheads and stuff. We never did see any of these finds, but that didn't matter, it was a great place for adventures anyway.

The main trunk was covered with many initials, some of them quite old. Tony had carved his own on there a couple of years earlier and TH 1954 was still clearly visible. We decided to climb up onto one of the lower boughs and add our own initials. Both of us carried penknives, most boys did at that time. We made ourselves comfortable on a nice fat bough, which we straddled, legs dangling and facing each other some six feet apart.

We whittled and chipped away for half an hour, by which time we had completed four inch high initials. I was quite pleased with my effort and so was David. We carefully edged past each other to look at the other's work. I had carved DH for Danny Haines and David had carved DH for himself.

- *Plenty of chestnuts around last that year.*

"How are people going to know who is who?"

"Well....your initials are nearest the trunk and mine are over here", I replied in all seriousness!

The return trip was uneventful and, just for a change, we went back round Alfie Hobbs' orchard and up the little lane by old George Beavan's house. When we emerged back onto the Green, which was a triangular piece of common land about 100 yards long each side, we saw George cutting fern with a hook. He was harvesting the stuff and drying it off for bedding. It was a common enough practice, albeit quite uncomfortable for the animals that had to lie on it. He looked up and saw we were peeling chestnuts.

"Give us some of them nuts then".

"Go and fetch yer own", replied David.

Clearly this boy was going to go a long way!

Father turned the radio on just before five o'clock. He always looked a lot more optimistic at that time, although his collar-less shirt and baggy corduroy trousers did leave a lot to be desired regarding sartorial elegance. His tall, gangly frame, together with high cheekbones and sunken eyes, made him look older than his 46 years. He sharpened a pencil into the fireplace, using one of Mother's best knives, then plonked himself down into one of the worn leather armchairs.

"I don't know what the world is coming to", said Mother as she bustled around in the front room, "we've got Russians invading Hungary and our own boys fighting the Egyptians, there'll be another World War you know.."

Father didn't answer, his favourite music had just started, it was the prelude to the football results. The end of his pencil danced to the tune as he waited with the newspaper folded neatly on his lap.

The first few results were noted down without a change in his expression but, as the illusive draws seemed to be everywhere except on his coupon, the optimism faded visibly. He screwed up his copy, tossed it onto the fire and looked forward to a pint down at the Greyhound.

I came into the room and emptied out the remaining chestnuts onto the table. There were still plenty of them left.

"You want to roast some of 'em", remarked Father, "just pop a handful in the oven".

Mother looked over the top of her glasses, said nothing but noted the pencil sharpening activity in the grate. Well, given that sort of 'all clear', I hooked open the heavy metal door and placed a double handful of nuts on the bottom of the oven.

Father wrestled a collar stud into position, fashioned some sort of knot in his tie and shouted a cheery 'goodbye' as he pulled on his coat and opened the door. Bob opened one eye briefly then closed it again; the dog and Father had an uneasy relationship. I think it all went back to when our old terrier 'Half Pint' had bitten him when he tried to take a rat out of his mouth. It hadn't been a very wise move and the wound had taken a long time to heal.

The peaceful silence was suddenly broken with a tremendous bang. Bob thought it was a shotgun and, as he was terrified of guns, raced out through the half open door and up towards the cowshed as fast as his legs would carry him.

"What on earth is that?", yelled Mother from the kitchen.

"I think the oven has exploded".

Mother raced in as another bang resounded across the room.

"Get those bloody chestnuts out of the oven will you", she snapped, "I don't know what your Father was thinking of".

I removed the exploding chestnuts as quickly as I could. Apparently they would have been a lot quieter if I had jabbed them like sausages. Well I didn't know that and anyway they still tasted really good, although you had to juggle them for a minute or two before they were cool enough to break open the shells. Generally the inner skin came away with the outer shell and that made it a lot less fiddling job to get them ready for eating. As I munched away I found myself wondering if David Holder was at home experiencing the delights of roast chestnuts.

It was Sunday the following day, a much more relaxed time on the farm with basically just the milking and mucking out to be done. We had just about finished when a strange car bounced its way up the track to the farmhouse. It was my eldest brother Dave, he had acquired a new car; new to him that was. It was a beaten up looking Austin Ruby which had replaced the AJS motorbike in his affections. He backed it down to the cowshed where Harold, Tony and I gathered around to inspect it.

Dave jumped out and looked as pleased as Punch; the new job as a maintenance fitter at the Mitcheldean BAF factory had meant a good pay-rise, part of which had gone on the car. His wife Pat was still at home with their daughter Sue who was just at the walking stage. He had a devil-may-care look about him with his black curly hair and twinkling eyes, although his appearance belied the fact that he was a right handful. For some reason he had not pursued a promising amateur boxing career when he returned from Korea, where a harsh two and a half years had done nothing to diminish his zest for life. If he could just have channelled as much energy into staying on the right side of the law as he seemed to spent trying to break it, he would have gone a long way. As it was he just couldn't stop poaching; nearly every weekend he was away with Tony and me, or some other ne'r-do-well mate.

"What do you think of my little buggy then?"

"Not bad", replied Harold, "you stopping or just calling by?"

"Well.....I was going to wash it down...I thought I could use some of that detergent from in the dairy".

"I thought there would be a catch", said Harold smiling and shaking his head as he walked away.

When he had finished washing down the Austin with the free detergent, hot water and brushes, Dave called us over.

"Come and see what I've got".

Tony and I went over to the car and he pulled out something from under the passenger seat. It was wrapped in an old cloth which was carefully unfolded to reveal a handgun.

"What sort is it?", asked Tony.

"A double-barrelled 410 shotgun pistol".

My God, we already had Father's old Navy 38 revolver and Dave's Army 45 automatic pistol in the house....now we had this as well!

It was a beauty though; a hammer action one with barrels about 16 inches long. A more deadly thing it was hard to imagine. Dave stuck it under his jacket and all three of us sneaked over to the small field, past the greengage trees and on to where a sheet of corrugated zinc had been used to repair a gap in the hedge.

"Let's see what the spread is like", said Dave as he popped in two cartridges and snapped the gun to the closed position. He cocked one hammer, took aim from six or seven yards and fired. It made the same racket as a normal 410 shotgun and it also punched quite a hole in the zinc. Tony had a go from further away and I had a go from close-up. The thing had quite a kick and your arm flew up into the air as you fired.

When we had finished messing about, Dave had calculated that he could pot pheasants from up to ten yards away. His cunning plan was to drive around quiet Cotswold lanes and blast anything perched on a wall or near the side of the road. What a toe-rag he was!

The recent Foot and Mouth outbreak had hit the Forest of Dean quite badly. Many thousands of animals had been slaughtered in an attempt to minimise the spread. Our neighbour, Henry Boughton, had lost a flock of 51 sheep as well as 19 heifers. But then, in the aftermath of this crisis, a major row had broken out.

It seemed that a large number of carcasses had been dumped into disused pit-shafts. That must have seemed an attractive low cost option at the time, but now the newspapers were questioning the risk to water supplies. It appeared that many of the old pits were flooded and there was a possible health risk with underground streams finding their way to goodness knows where. The idea of decomposing animals in your water supply was not something you liked to dwell on. To make it worse, it seemed that no one had obtained permission to dump carcasses in the first place. However, after a little while all the furore died down and the problem quietly faded away. By then Christmas was almost upon us and we had the poultry to pluck, dress and deliver. There was never time to dwell on anything for very long.

Harold had saved the really big turkeys until last. The ducks and cockerels were already nicely dressed and labelled for delivery. He had learned from bitter experience that stunning one of these huge stags was followed by a furious flapping of wings. If you lost your grip at that stage they could easily break your arm.

The plucking was not easy either. The large wing feathers were a devil of a job to get out and fingers were pretty sore after a couple of days of it.

"Who is this new bloke taking over the King's Head then?", asked Tony through a haze of down feathers.

"His name is Bert Cole", replied Harold.

"What's he like?"

"Okay they reckon".

They pressed on until the last bird was finished; it was a wonderful moment, one to be savoured with a nice Players Navy Cut.

They didn't use Violet and the float for the deliveries any more; the battered old Land Rover now provided a quicker and warmer means of doing the job. It also had the benefit that Harold couldn't have too many drinks from well-wishers, a problem that had occurred from time to time with the horse-drawn deliveries!

It was good to have that annual blitz activity behind us and were all able to relax a bit. Christmas Day started quite brightly at first but then the sky turned an odd steely grey colour. Just a few flakes fell at first then gradually became rather heavy. We did indeed have a very white Christmas that year.

Lightly Poached

Chapter Four
Early 1957

We rarely referred to our father as Dad; most of the time we called him Father or, on a very bad day, it might be something else. Dave and Tony called him 'our old chap' when he wasn't around. It wasn't that he was that miserable, it was just that somewhere along the line he had lost the ability to have a damn good laugh. However, he was willing to have a go at something new and, when Father got an idea into his head, it was hard to shift it. This time he wanted to take me from Cinderford into Gloucester on the train. I didn't mind at all, in fact it sounded rather good; the one and only time I had been on a train before had been three years earlier when Father, Tony and I had gone down to Southampton to meet Dave on his return from Korea.

• *The entrance to the old East Dean Grammar School hasn't changed much in the last 50 years.*

It was during the school holidays when we caught the bus up to Cinderford and got off by the Picture House. They were showing *'Genevieve'*, a far too soppy film for my liking. The trip was a bit like the routine of going to school except we went on past the entrance to East Dean and kept going down Station Street. I glanced at the long red brick building in which I now seemed to spend most of my daylight hours. Some of the brickwork was crumbling and the railings around the school yard needed a lick of paint. We walked for another two hundred yards down to the aptly named Railway Inn and then turned right in through the entrance to the station.

It was either by brilliant planning, or else very good luck, that the train arrived soon after. The weather was bleak and patches of snow remained where drifts had formed a few days earlier. Our breath was clearly visible and you could feel the cold air in your nostrils. I was glad to be in long trousers at last and, with my thick blue overcoat and scarf, felt I could face anything the Winter could throw at me.

The train came to a halt amidst much hissing and squealing; plumes of white smoke and steam swirled together and seemed to cloak the entire station. There weren't many people waiting on the platform that day and minutes later we were aboard. We eased our way out of the station and around the severe bend to rejoin the main track.

It was all rather exciting to be weaving our way through the Forest on a train, gently rocking and swaying as the track-side trees flew by in a blurred continuous stream. I fiddled with the leather strap operating the window and generally mooched about to my heart's content. We went through a couple of short tunnels which took me rather by surprise.

"You'd better sit down old butt, we shall be going through the big tunnel soon".

"Well how big is it?"

"It'll take us several minutes to go though it".

As I sat down he took out his 'baccy'. It was in an old 2oz Golden Virginia tin with a large piece of potato peel inside to help keep the tobacco moist.

"Fancy one?"

"Not half", I replied eagerly.

Father pulled a paper from a Rizla packet and took a small pinch of tobacco; he then motioned me to do the same. He rolled the mixture expertly, ran the tip of his tongue along the gummed edge and sealed it. He pinched the dangling bits from either end and placed it in his mouth. My attempt was amateurish but adequate. Father struck a Swan Vesta and offered it up to me. I took a few good puffs to get it going and tried to look as if I was enjoying it. I felt a burning sensation in my throat but I was determined not to cough or look anything but happy. Bringing up a lad in those days included teaching him to smoke, drink and swear, as well as doing a fair proportion of the chores.

Soon after we entered the Haie tunnel which, when built in 1809, was the longest railway tunnel in the world. And, as we rocked and rolled our way through it, Father recalled an event that had taken place when he was just a young lad. He had been born in Newnham and, together with three other boys, regularly played on the track and in the tunnel. They had become more and more daring and decided one day to go right through to the other end.

There were many small alcoves in the tunnel wall where they were able to flatten themselves if a train was coming. All four of them set off to ride their luck; the danger and doing what they knew they shouldn't was the big attraction. Their eyes became accustomed to the darkness and they shouted and sang at the top of their voices, safe in the knowledge that no one could hear them. After a quarter of an hour or so they heard the unmistakable sound of a train approaching. They raced to find alcoves but one of them was too slow. In that moment of terror and indecision, the train hit him. He was killed outright of course; there would be no more playing in the big tunnel......

The train came to a noisy halt in Newnham Station. Father tapped my arm.

"Come on then.....we change here".

We hurried along the carriage, down the steps and onto the platform. Father told me to stay where I was while he went off and spoke to someone. When he returned he looked rather pleased with himself.

"Come on....we're going to have a look at the engine".

He set off towards the front of the train and I followed closely behind. The driver and the fireman both turned, smiled at me and spoke. Father helped me up onto the footplate. I couldn't hear a word they were saying but their sweat-streaked faces were kind and their blackened hands used to hard work. The fireman carried on shovelling coal onto the roaring fire through a small metal door which he had opened with the end of his shovel. It was an incredible experience to be up in the front of a steam train; although any schoolboy plans to be an engine driver were somewhat dented by all the smoke and din.

Soon after, we stepped back down onto the platform and waited for the connecting train. It wasn't long before it arrived and we were grateful to hop on board and grab some seats in the warm once more. We hurtled along past Westbury and Minsterworth with occasional plumes of smoke billowing by the windows; it was a view I had seen many times from the top of Chestnuts Wood.

The train rattled on along with the repetitive 'rat-a-tat-tat' as we ate up the miles of track. The thought flashed through my mind of Royston Wellington and his run in with our old headmaster, Mr Meek, over expansion joints. I smiled to myself as I gazed out through the window but, before I knew it, we were slowing down to enter Gloucester station. It was a lot busier there; people were walking purposefully in all directions and I stuck close to Father as he headed out through the exit.

He took me across the road and into the Wellington pub. He hadn't taken me into a pub before and I felt a bit awkward in there. Thank goodness he didn't buy me a half of bitter and offer me another roll-up.

I sipped a glass of pop while he downed a couple of pints. Then, suitably refreshed, he searched out a fish and chip shop. We ate the piping hot food directly out of the newspaper as we strolled steadily towards King's Square. We polished off the last of the chips, tossed the wrapping paper in a bin and, after a short wait, caught the Red and White bus home.

We got off at Denton's Corner where Father disappeared over the gate into Henry Boughton's field with unseemly haste. He reappeared minutes later looking much relieved and we walked on up Watery End Lane towards Mrs Baldwin's cottage. Her nasty wall-eyed dog flung itself against the wire fence, snarling and barking furiously.

"Bloody thing", said Father, trying to light a roll-up as he spoke.

The dog had just about stopped barking as we neared Nelly Powell's house up on the Common. That was the signal for her dog 'Cuddly' to leap on the wall and start making a racket. How that creature ever got called 'Cuddly' I would never understand. Dave had threatened to shoot it and I was always fearful that one day he would carry it out. Nevertheless, it had been a great day and I would always remember the sights and sounds of the Forest railway. We did not know it at the time, but the railway did not have long to go; kids in the future would not have the same opportunity to stare into the roaring fire of a steam train or to rattle along the tree-lined Forest tracks.

A couple of ton of sugar beet had been unloaded by the far end of the new cowshed. We had two cowsheds by that time, each able to hold eight cows for milking. We had also acquired a hand operated grater, as the cattle were not very keen on munching the hard beet unless it had been chopped up. The grater had originally been bright red and olive green, but was now somewhat faded, chipped and rusty. It worked perfectly well nevertheless, the large rotary shredding disc responded well to a brisk turn of the handle.

Tony wore no cap that wintry morning, but he did have two pullovers on to keep out the biting wind, and wellingtons to negotiate the mud by the cowshed and the track leading on down to the Orchard. He stacked a couple of dozen of the coconut-sized beet into the grater basket and took a good grip on the handle. His hand was soon moving in a two foot circular motion and, as speed built up, a steady flow of finely shredded beet fell into the wheelbarrow placed under the exit chute. Several years of manual operation of the sheep shearing machine had taught Tony the benefit of keeping up a nice steady even pace, and not to go mad at it.

When the barrow was full, he took it round to the cowsheds and scooped out a bowl-full to each animal. They were more than grateful and hungrily set about their sweet, moist treat. As they ate, steam from their backs rose slowly upwards and condensed on the cold corrugated roof. Droplets then formed which ran down the underside of the roof and eventually dripped off the galvanised bolts and back down onto the animals below.

Tony carried a metal bucket into the dairy where he part filled it with cold water and then topped it up from the boiler. He tested it, found it to be a little on the cool side and so added more hot water. A clean cloth was tossed into the bucket as he headed off into the new cowshed. Harold had already started milking in the original, or 'old' cowshed as it was called.

He went to Rosie, a Friesian at the end of the shed. She completely ignored him as he washed her teats with the cloth and warm water; it would have been a very different story of course if he had used ice-cold water instead. Jennifer was in the next stall and her teats were washed in the same way; both Rosie and Jennifer were far more interested in the fodder beet and cow-cake than they ever were in Tony. He took the first of his two milking machines and pushed the flexible air hose onto the air supply. It hissed as the connection was made, then started its relentless and repetitive slurping noise as the four milking machine 'hands' contracted and released with the controlled pulses of compressed air.

Those mechanical 'hands' would slurp onto a teat much like a hungry young calf; within seconds all four 'hands' were engaged and the flow of milk could be seen in the small viewing window. The second machine was put onto Jennifer and Tony took the opportunity to light up a Players Navy Cut.

Harold sometimes lit a brazier on very cold mornings. The brazier was a rather grand name for an old bucket with some holes punched in it, but on a freezing morning you were unlikely to worry much about that. He had lit one that morning and Tony went over to the old cowshed for a warm. He rubbed his hands close to the flames and enjoyed the warmth with his cigarette held in clenched teeth.

"There's boxing down at the Unlawater next week", he remarked as he removed the cigarette with care, "do you fancy going?"

Harold's head appeared up over the top of Gertrude's back.

"Ay...wouldn't mind....why don't you ask Dave?"

We had all maintained a keen interest in boxing, although Dave himself had not pursued his own earlier ABA ambitions. I had got up with Father at 4' o clock in the

• *Tony carrying a bale of hay on a wintery morning.*

morning on a number of occasions to listen to world championship fights on the radio. When I was still at Littledean School, I had listened to Ezzard Charles and Don Cockell put up brave performances before the relentless Rocky Marciano caught up with them. I still had to be up again, just a few hours later, and off to school. However, at a local level there were often bouts staged at the Unlawater Hotel in Newnham-on-Severn, and that was only a couple of miles down the road.

Tony said he would check with Dave if he saw him during the week, and then headed back to check his two milking machines. The flow of milk through the viewing windows was down to a trickle; it was time to move the machines onto fresh udders.

When a milking machine bucket was full, the heavy milking attachment was unclipped and transferred to an empty spare bucket. That was quickly slurped onto the next udder and the full one carried to the dairy for cooling.

It was important to cool the milk rapidly and not to leave it to the elements. This was true in Winter just as much as Summer. We had a cooler which worked by cascading the warm milk down over a water-chilled corrugated surface. The corrugation ensured that the cascading milk was in contact with the cold surface for as long as possible. The chilled milk was then transferred to churns for collection by 'Blear's Dairy' from Drybrook.

The routine of milking nearly 30 cows was repeated twice daily, once before breakfast and again just before tea. It was a repetitive job, but it was the one that paid most of the bills.

A little later that morning, Tony took the pitchfork from the cowshed and wandered around to the barn. The level of the hay bales had dropped considerably. The early cold snap and hanging snow had necessitated a lot of supplementary feeding of the animals. He selected a bale, jabbed the fork in hard and swung it up onto his shoulder. The barn door was closed behind him with a flick of his wellington boot, leaving a muddy size eight footprint on it as he did so.

Bob looked at him questioningly. He wasn't sure whether or not to stay with Harold who was still busy with the cleaning out. He was very loyal to Harold and followed him everywhere. On this occasion Tony made his mind up for him.

"Come on boy", he shouted, "let's go and feed them there sheep".

Bob was still as keen as mustard; he raced off in front, then came back for a moment, and was off again. My word that dog burned off some sort of energy; he never seemed to walk one mile when he could run three or four! They headed off down the track towards the Pike House. It was owned by Mr George Phelps, who lived there with his wife and daughter, Pam. As its name suggests, it was a place where travellers were once levied for tax, the amount depended on the goods they were carrying. Whenever I saw Mr Phelps he always seemed to be carrying two buckets suspended from a wooden yoke across his shoulders. He seemed to be permanently ferrying stuff between the house and the sheds, carefully balancing the buckets as they dangled on their chains.

There was no sign of him that morning however, the snow and sharp wind saw to that. Bob raced straight across the George Lane without looking; Tony's head was bent and he was now staring at his toe-caps under the ever increasing weight of the hay bale. Luckily there were no cars around and no harm was done.

When he reached the gate to the Lower Grove, Tony lobbed the bale straight over it and waited a moment or two for the indentation to go out of his shoulder. He cursed silently and rubbed his frozen hands to get the circulation going. Bob scrabbled between the lower bars of the gate and looked back as if egging Tony to hurry up. The flock of Scottish Black-face ewes found themselves caught between hunger and fear. They desperately wanted to get at the hay, but were very wary of the dog.

Eventually both man and dog were reunited on the far side of the gate. Tony jabbed the fork into the ground for safe keeping, then carried the bale the last few yards to the feeding racks. He took out his knife, slashed the strings, and pulled them clear before winding them up and putting them in his jacket pocket.

The hay was shaken into the top of the feeding racks, spread around a little and the rain-proof lids hinged back down. Most of the ewes were eating by this time and only a few were still standing back warily.

The Black-face sheep were a hardy breed and well adapted to harsh Winters out on exposed hills. We had acquired them for just that reason; the Upper Grove comprised 17 acres of very hilly and rough grazing, with plenty of gorse and bramble to negotiate. However, they would come down off the hill and tackle hay quite readily; this was unlike some of the Welsh mountain sheep that would rather starve to death than eat hay and save themselves.

Tony put a cigarette in his mouth, cupped his hands and lit up. Two or three good puffs went up into the cold morning air as he looked over the sheep. They all seemed to be fine but he knew, in a couple of months or so, the lambing season would bring its usual combination of joy and heartbreak.

"Come on boy, let's get on back"

Bob leapt forward, his tongue dangling in and out of his mouth in rapid fashion as he gulped in more air. This time he was at heel when they got back to the George Lane, where Tony glanced left and right before giving him the go ahead to cross. The dog was already back with Harold by the time Tony reached the Big Meadow gate.

Lightly Poached

Chapter Five
Spring 1957

The Winter had been hard. Animals needed daily hay and supplementary food for much of the time and we had all but run out. The Apple Meadow and Big Meadow barns were empty, and there was no more than a couple of dozen bales left in the main barn. If the milder weather had not arrived in April, we would have been buying extra hay at top price. As it was the soft ground had been quickly chewed up by cloven hooves as the animals searched out every blade of new grass.

It was our seventh Winter on the farm and each one brought a new set of problems. The latest was that our old Ferguson tractor was becoming increasingly difficult to get going first thing, and now had to be parked outside on a steep hill for bump starting. Although the metal seat on the tractor hinged back to allow rain to drain off, it was still a bit of a shock to your backside first thing in the morning. It was even worse if you forgot to hinge it back the night before and had to scrape the snow off first!

Alfie Hobbs had come over and knocked on the door a couple of weeks earlier. This was quite rare; he only lived just across the Common but tended to keep himself to himself. His father, who we only ever knew as 'Scritchie', needed Harold to have a look at a ewe that was having trouble yeaning. 'Scritchie' could never have made it up along the Common himself, he had very bad rheumatism and only got about with a pair of old long-handled brooms under his armpits.

It was a white, frosty morning when I accompanied Tony and Harold down to 'Scritchie's' small plum orchard. Inevitably we had to endure the racket of 'Cuddly', Nellie Powell's awful dog.

"Shut tha up", hissed Tony.

I watched the overweight collie run up and down the garden wall. The dog had never worked with sheep and was by then too fat to chase them anyway. It made up for that by making a noise....a lot of noise.

The Hobbs family kept 20 or so ewes; they were let out to graze on Common land during the Summer, but were kept in their orchard over the Winter months. Harold untied some frayed bailing string that secured an old wooden gate to a drunken looking

• *Harold delivers the lamb with Tony and me holding the ewe nice and still.*

gatepost and then wrestled it open. The orchard looked like a Christmas card; the bare plum trees were still covered in frost and glistened in the weak sunlight. Alf was waiting just inside and thanked Harold warmly for coming to his aid so quickly. They looked an unlikely pair; Harold was a stocky five foot eight whereas Alf was at least six foot six and gangly with it. He was a really pleasant chap, rather quiet and courteous but had to endure countless jokes about his big feet. Tony reckoned that with his size 14's he should have played in goal for the Rovers.

The sight that greeted us was a grim one. The ewes were not penned and most of them already had lambs. The very young ones looked all legs as they raced to their mothers to suckle, their doomed little tails waggling furiously as they did so. One was in obvious trouble however, and it didn't take more than a few seconds to see why. She was walking around with her bowel heaved out. The lamb was presumably breached and she had been heaving most of the night, eventually doing awful damage to herself.

"Alf....go and get half a bucket of warm water, some soap and a clean piece of cloth", instructed Harold, "Tone...let's catch her as easy as we can".

Bob had been left at home; there was no rounding up to be done and it reduced the possibility of the remaining pregnant ewes being made to run unnecessarily. We coaxed the ewe, together with a few others, into a makeshift pen that Alf and his father had built in the corner of the orchard. In there it was fairly easy to catch her; Tony held her tightly as Harold took a closer look.

"What do you reckon?"

Harold looked at the exposed bowel which was hanging out like a large bunch of grapes. There was bits of frost and small debris on the exposed area where the poor thing had lay down repeatedly to try to give birth.

"Well...it don't look very good".

Just then Alf returned with the warm water; Harold tested it with his fingers, it was a little too hot but he knew it would cool quickly.

"Let's have her over then".

I helped Tony turn her over so as to minimise her struggling. We lay her on her side and peered over as Harold dipped the cloth into the hot water. He held it up for a moment to let it cool then gently bathed the exposed area. He did this for several minutes to ensure that the bowel was clean and warm again. Then, with extreme care, he eased it back inside her. In fact it went back in without too much difficulty and that prompted Tony to speak.

"Well that wasn't so bad".

"Putting it back in aint the problem, it's keeping it there that matters, besides there's still a lamb in her somewhere".

Harold took off his heavy jacket, rolled up his shirt sleeve as high as he could up his right arm, and applied soap and water generously. He kneeled on the frosty ground and eased his hand inside the ewe. The lamb was big, breached and dead. It took him ages to turn it and then deliver it. He placed the dead lamb on the ground, wiped the frost off his knees and looked at the long suffering ewe.

"Let's get her up on her feet....nice and easy mind".

Harold took some baling string out of his pocket and tied it around the ewe's belly just in front of her back legs. He then took what looked like a quarter of a rabbit net and placed it around her rear end, under her tail, and secured it onto the 'belly string'. The hope was that it would keep the bowel in place while she recovered.

"Alf....tell thy father that she's lost the lamb and the next 24 hours will decide if she can keep that lot inside her. If not....she'll have to be put down".

Alf nodded his head but said nothing; we all knew she didn't have much of a chance. Harold was called back down the following evening; he took the lump hammer and a good knife with him. The ewe had been given every chance, but by then she needed to be put out of her misery.

Father was very grateful for the milder weather; the long Winter walk to the village every morning to catch the Gloucester bus had been grim. Padding along the George Lane through snow and slush had not done his shoes or his sense of humour a lot of good. Every evening when he got home there was a wavy white line halfway up his shoes where the salty water had penetrated the leather. They were leaned up against the fender, dried during the evening, and another good coating of brown polish applied just before he went to bed.

The increase in temperature had also coaxed some Spring flowers out of their Winter hiding; it also brought ice-creams back onto the agenda.

"Do'st thee fancy an ice-cream?" asked Father sternly.

"Well ay", I replied on behalf of myself and Tony, who were both doing nothing that Sunday morning.

"Right then...I'll get some money".

Father disappeared inside to get his wallet while Tony and I scuffed some shoes on without bending down to ease the heels in. Minutes later we were heading along the George Lane in the direction of Littledean. We didn't look particularly smart, our pullovers had holes in the elbows and my old shoes hadn't seen polish in many a week. It didn't really matter and we didn't worry much about our appearance anyway.

We seemed to pick up speed a bit as we cut up through the Folders Estate. My attention was taken by a thrush that was desperately trying to crack open a snail on some stony ground. I was still looking back at it when Jim Giles appeared in the doorway of his house.

- *A song thrush hard at work cracking a snail-shell.*

"Where are you beggars off to?"

"Going to get some ice-creams", I replied.

"I should think thee bist", said Jim as he turned on his heels and went back in. Bernard Giles came running out to the gate as we moved on up the road.

"Can I have one of them ice-creams?", he shouted in a pleading sort of voice.

"No you bloody can't", replied Tony, and turning to me added, "an' keep your big trap shut in future".

I thought of the implications of further sharing a one and sixpenny block of ice-cream and realised the error of my ways. Soon after we arrived at the Post Office and General Store run by Tom Davis. It was shut of course on a Sunday morning, but we knew the secret access. Father opened a white, wooden side-door that was set in a high garden wall. We entered and closed the door quietly to keep out any prying eyes. A concrete path led to the back door of the house. Father tapped gently on it with one knuckle as if not wanted to disturb a late sleeper.

Within seconds Tom Davis appeared. He was a genial chap who seemed a bit ancient to a young lad like me; his short stature added to his portly appearance and there was not a lot of grey hair left on his head. He had the most enormous goitre on the back of his neck and it was hard not to stare at it. Several buttons were undone on the top of his shirt to keep it loose, and he held his head slightly on one side like someone with a stiff neck.

"Morning Henry, I see you've got the family with you today".

"Ay...well most of 'em anyway", replied Father glancing in the direction of Tony and

• *The dreaded cross-country race.*

me, then added, "can we have a block of vanilla, some wafers and a knife please".

Tom nodded, turned on his heels and went back inside. He emerged a minute later carrying an enormous block of ice-cream. We had learned the benefit of bulk buying during the previous Summer; a one and sixpenny block could be cut into six decent sized pieces. Father took the knife and cut the block with incredible care and precision; there was never any need to look for the biggest slice as they were all going to be exactly the same. He eased the end slice away slightly and placed a wafer either side of it. My mouth was open by then and I was drooling the way Bob did whenever he heard toast being scrunched. He handed the first one to me, thankfully, and I rasped my tongue up both the long sides before taking my first bite. It tasted every bit as good as it looked, and we polished off one each while Father talked to Tom about the shortcomings of the parish council and generally put the rest of the world to rights. We then had one more each on the way home. It was a very pleasant way to spend an hour on a Sunday morning, that is if lunch wasn't too early!

My old friend Royston Wellington had gone. It seemed that his parent's marriage had broken up and his mother had taken him to live somewhere in Somerset. Royston had never talked about it and there had been no gossip or speculation in the village. One day he was at school and the next day he was gone. It was a big shock to me; there was no goodbye and I never saw him again.

Meanwhile, I had heard some of the older lads at school talking about the cross-country run, and what they said wasn't very nice at all. Soon after we had a double PE lesson and Mr Goddard instructed us to get changed into shorts, rugby top and no socks. I just knew what was to follow; we were marched down Station Street, past the Gas Works, across Valley Road and onto a wide Forestry track. We walked on for a further hundred yards and stopped on the Letchers railway bridge. I leaned on the safety fence and looked down onto the gleaming rails below. The track seemed more curved than I thought it would and it went as far as I could see in either direction. For a few seconds I forgot what lay ahead.

"Okay you lot, just stick with the older boys, they know the route and that way you won't get lost", said the loveable Mr G.

There was a five mile senior course and a three mile junior one. I was running the junior course for the first time, and some seniors were sent round with us on that first run to generally look after us.

We formed a ragged, three deep line of about 50 of us in all. There was every size and shape of white leg dangling from navy blue shorts.

"Ready.....get set.....go".

Off we went; the pace was far too fast to start with. After a few hundred yards we reached the edge of the Crump Meadow gypsy camp. It was not a place for the faint-hearted.

"Come on you lot at the back.....keep up", yelled one of the seniors.

I could see why; there were dozens of caravans and tents, each one seemed to have a snarling dog or a youngster happy to sling pebbles at what they considered to be a bunch of idiots. They were a rough and ready lot, there was no way you wanted to be travelling alone through that part of the wood. We managed to circle the camp in a tight pack, a bit like a shoal of fish hoping safety in numbers would save them from a predator.

Just when you started to feel safe from attack, you then hit the next problem. It was a small brook with a steep bank either side. The more athletic lads would leap from one bank and land halfway up the other side like a graceful salmon. For the rest of us it was a formidable barrier; if you didn't clear the water, then you ran the rest of the race with wet feet. Mr Goddard had thoughtfully made us run without socks; that at least ensured we had something dry to put on our feet when it was all over.

I approached the ditch gasping for air. Behind me, the gypsies' dogs were just about settling down again. I took a good run at it, took off too early, and landed in the mud at the bottom of the far bank.

"Oh bugger it all", I cursed as I scrambled up the bank, leaving one dap behind as I did so.

My bare foot got plastered in mud as I tried to hop back and retrieve it. Meanwhile, the rest of the 'tail-enders' were landing all around me like hippos, throwing up mud and water in all directions.

The next two and a half miles were truly exhausting. I found that being relatively strong from farm work was not much use on a cross-country run. Eventually it came to a merciful end. Mr Goddard, who I never did see run further than across a classroom, waited by the starting point to count us all back in. This training continued for several weeks, and on rainy days there no socks, just cold, wet feet.

Two terms at East Dean had been long enough to forge some lasting friendships. The nucleus of a gang of like-minded lads was beginning to form. Some drifted in and out of this group for a time but remained mates over the years. If you saw any one of these lads, the chance was that he would be with a couple of the other 'members'. The initial group included David Holder, Dave 'Benny' Bennett, Dave Meek and Antony Meek, who were known as Meek D and Meek A in daily registration, as well as 'Flowery' Roberts, John 'Younger' Young and myself. Others would over time join this select group who had a number of things in common. These included being reasonably bright but unwilling to work very hard, not being keen on authority and finally, not on Mr Goddard's Christmas card list!

We tended to stick together outside the classroom and this extended to cross country training. One day we hung towards the back of the pack by the gypsy camp. That did not rouse much interest as we tended to drift to the back anyway. As we approached a small fir plantation on the left, David Holder spoke.

"Come on.....in here...quick!"

I looked around, no-one was looking, so I followed him in closely followed by 'Benny' and the Meeks.

"Let's have a breather", gasped Antony, his usually white pallor now an angry red and his muddy knees looking more knobbly than ever.

'Benny' and Dave Meek were heavier framed than the rest of us and unsuited to Mr Goddard's punishment. We all slumped down onto the grass as we got our breath back and then began to laugh nervously.

"I 'ent doing no more cross country runs", said David Holder, his confidence soaring with our initial success at skiving.

"No nor me.......sod 'em", added 'Benny' with an expression that suggested he meant it.

We stayed there for about a quarter of an hour, or so it seemed; none of us had a watch and so we couldn't be very precise about it.

"Come on......let's make our way through to the Foxes Bridge track", suggested David Holder.

It seemed a reasonable idea. We cut through the small fir plantation and circled the gypsy camp, keeping a good distance from it and their dogs. Eventually we reached the track; it was about 600 yards from the finish, although that was around the next bend and we couldn't see it. We looked up and down; there was no-one in sight.

"We've left it too late......come on", shouted Dave Meek as he burst out of the undergrowth and onto the track.

"Come on...", he repeated.

We followed quickly, still in a group formation, and jogged down to the finish where Mr Goddard was stood with a couple of lads who had sick notes. He had a nasty expression on his face and a large dap in his right hand which he was hitting gently onto his other palm.

"Run quicker than usual did you?"

"Yes sir......that was the best we've done so far sir", I added, still a bit confused why he should ask such a strange question.

"You'll all be delighted to know that you have just managed to take the first five places today", said Mr G; his eyes narrowed to slits as he said, "bend over Haines".

He gave me six whacks with the dap; really hard ones that hurt like hell, although none of us were going to show anything in front of the others. One by one my mates all got the same treatment; by the end of the session Mr Goddard was tiring, 'Benny' was lucky, he was the last in line.

"Okay....so you like running fast do you.....well try running around again, and if you cheat this time you'll be up in front of the Headmaster".

We headed back towards the gypsy camp once more. They stared at us vacantly as we started our second lap; you should have heard the names we called Mr G!

The training continued over the next couple of weeks under the vigilant eye of our beloved Games Master. Eventually, the day of the final arrived. The weather was kind for once; it was a bright sort of day and reasonably dry under foot. We were instructed to get changed into our House colours. Red was Drake, blue was Hawkins and yellow was Raleigh. The cross country event had a team prize as well as an individual one. I was in Drake House and donned my bright-red rugby-style shirt ready for the off.

We trooped down Station Street, looked in through the window of the Railway Inn at the customers enjoying their liquid lunch, and reluctantly moved on to the starting point for the race. The lads with sick notes to excuse them from the forthcoming agony had all been sent on ahead to act as markers. They were stationed in pairs all around both the junior and senior courses, and instructed to count the number of runners. This had the effect of checking for any 'short cuts' that might be taken, as well as any injuries from dog or catapult attacks, or even a twisted ankle.

Mr Goddard lined us up and, after a long wait which allowed us plenty of time to ponder on what lay ahead, he eventually fired his starting pistol. We tore off at an incredible pace and I was knackered after 200 yards. No-one was talking very much as it took every bit of breath just to keep up. I looked around and saw 'Benny', 'Flowery' and 'Younger' gasping nearby; we kept close order as we reached the gypsy camp. It was their 'carnival day'; the young ragamuffins threw sticks and laughed as their dogs hurled themselves at us, only the tethering ropes and chains stopped us being ripped to pieces.

A few future Olympic stars vanished into the distance, but the rest of us kept together in a pack, jogging along a barely tolerable pace. We followed a narrow Forestry track for another three quarters of a mile, passing through pleasant woodland until we came to an old disused railway line. There was a small stile nearby, but arriving in a pack meant that most of us opted to jump the fence on either side of it. A length of barbed wire had been thoughtfully strung along the top of the posts. I managed to keep my hands clear of the barbs but slipped as I jumped down the other side. Unfortunately, my shorts snagged on the wire and there was a loud tearing noise as I landed. I checked the damage; there was a huge 'L' shaped rent in my shorts and a long cut on my bum. It was bleeding quite badly but no-one cared; it was everyone for himself. If someone had dropped down on the side of the track, he would have been left for the markers to find him, and besides, it meant you hadn't come last!

After a bad bout of stitch that slowed me down for a while, I did get a second wind and ran on quite well after that. I overtook quite a few down the long clinker path from Foxes Bridge, although what they must have thought of my bare backside I have no idea. On we went until with enormous gratitude we reached the last bend before the finishing straight. It was then I saw them. The entire female population of East Dean were lined up three deep either side of the finish. As I got to about 50 yards from it I grabbed the back of my flapping shorts to hide my bleeding posterior.

I can tell you that being utterly exhausted and running along swinging only one arm, was awful. As I neared the line I heard Gaynor Holford shouting "come on Daa....nee, come on Daa....nee".

Behind me, Derek Stevens was closing fast; he could swing both arms and sensed he could catch me. I just couldn't let go of my shorts in front of all those girls; we finished almost together, Derek was 7th and I was in 8th place.

When the last of the runners were all in we were allowed to walk back up to the school; in my case still holding my torn shorts. I vowed to be a marker in future years even if I had to get our Dave to forge an 'excuse note' on medical grounds; I'd think of something!

• *Harold and Tony tailing the lambs*

Chapter Six
Summer 1957

Memories of the agonising cross-country race faded slowly over the weeks that followed; by then we had our full complement of lambs running free up in the Grove. However, it was time for tailing and castrating them and, fortunately, we had just acquired the latest tool for the job. There would be no more red-hot irons to cut off tails and seal the wounds, nor the crude pincer used to crush the tubes of the ram lambs. No, we had got an Elastrator; a simple tool that stretched a small, bright-orange rubber ring over the tail or scrotum, where it was eased off and left. It was a tight fit that quickly cut off the blood flow making the area numb. Over the next few weeks the area under the rubber ring withered away completely and the tail or scrotum just fell off. The system had the advantage that there was little risk of infection as there were no open wounds. The reaction of the lambs also showed that the level of discomfort was minimal compared with that of a blade or a hot iron and pincers.

Harold and Tony strolled slowly over to the Grove with Bob zig-zagging out in front of them. The soft slapping noise of their wellingtons accompanied their every stride.

"Here boy!" shouted Harold as they approached the George Lane.

It was a blind spot in the direction of Littledean and Tony held the dog by the scruff of the neck until Harold walked halfway across and nodded that it was okay to release him. Bob raced ahead knowing that sheep chasing was only minutes away.

In a seventeen acre field, much of it hilly with patchy gorse and undergrowth, a sheep-dog was essential. On foot it would have taken an exhausting half an hour to get all the sheep and lambs down to the barn. However with the exuberant Bob in full flow it took less than five minutes to get them in and a hurdle placed across the entrance. The next job was to catch the ewes and turn them out. Harold opted to manage the hurdle, leaving the younger man to corner the Black-face one by one and wheel them out, one hand gripping the curved horns and the other a handful of wool on the rump. Bob did his level best to nip each one as she darted past him. Moments later, when at a safe distance, she would turn and bleat continuously to her lamb inside the barn.

Once all the ewes were outside, it made the job of catching the lambs much easier. It also meant they didn't have to watch their backs when aggressive mothers took exception to their young being manhandled. It was then time to start using the new tool for real. Tony grabbed a lamb and parked it with the rear end facing Harold. He slid the small rubber ring over the four expandable fingers of the application tool, squeezed the handles and slid the rubber ring up along the tail. When it was an inch or so from the rump he released the handles and eased the ring off onto the tail. There was no reaction at all from the lamb.

"Well that wasn't too bad", remarked Tony.

"No.....seemed painless didn't it", said Harold as he watched the youngster scamper off in the direction of her mother. The bleating between anxious mums and the remaining beleaguered young continued for half an hour, gradually reducing in volume until the last lamb was done.

"Time for a fag 'aint it?" said Tony in a questioning sort of way.

Harold placed the half empty box of Elastrator rings in his one jacket pocket and took his packet of Players out of the other. Without speaking he opened the packet and offered one to Tony.

"Ta", he said and snapped an old petrol lighter several times before it sprang into life.

"Thous need a new flint in that 'un", commented Harold as he lowered his cigarette down into the cupped hands that were protecting the black, smoky flame.

He took two good puffs and threw his head back as he inhaled.

"Ay....this Elastrator tool is damn good", he said to himself, breathing out the smoke as he did so.

The Summer was warm with the odd sprinkling of rain to keep the mowing grass growing nicely. It had become tall and swayed gently in the breeze giving the effect of rippling water. It had also become a bit of a temptation to a few youngsters from the village; they had climbed the gate into the Lower Grove and trampled their way to the middle of the field where they had great fun rolling around and flattening the grass.

"If I catch 'em I'll tan their asses", remarked Father.

"You do nothing of the sort.....you stay well away from them", instructed Mother. "If we find out who it is we'll go and see their parents and put a stop to it that way".

The look on Father's face indicated that he still believed his solution was best.

Luckily they didn't come back again and so confrontation was avoided. Soon after it was time for mowing anyway. The forecast was good for the next three days and Tony pressed on with the tractor and mower. Meanwhile I was back at school with double woodwork to look forward to.

The lessons one particular morning were all languages. First there was Latin with Mr Aveston. He was a stern looking middle-aged man with wavy, greying hair that reminded me of a sheet of corrugated zinc. There was no nonsense in his lessons at all. It usually took the first ten minutes to work out the date in Latin. I dreaded the days when he picked me for that difficult task. Each month had different parts in it; everyone has heard of the Ides of March for example, but there were plenty of others to have to remember. On top of that, sentence construction was all back to front, so even when you had worked out all the words you still had a devil of a job getting them in the correct order. If you finally got all that right, you still had to manage the pronunciation! Most 'V's' were pronounced like 'W's'; sometimes Mr Aveston sounded like he had a whole mouthful of 'W's'!

After that we had French. Miss Birde-Jones took us for that during the first year. She was a unusual character; a rather petite lady with shortish wavy brown hair. Her lips were rather thin with a smear of red lipstick applied carefully to them. I never saw her without her black gown wrapped around her shoulders. She would ask a question and then tell us to put our paw in the air if we knew the answer. We thought it was dreadfully daring, but that was as near as we ever came to humour from any of the teachers.

Finally it was time for double woodwork; Mr Fern took the lesson as usual with his friend 'Archibald' suspended up on the wall. We were part way through making a very simple tray with jointed end pieces with hand holes in them. I rather enjoyed woodwork; it was a pleasant change from the cold, humourless lessons that filled most days. I had to admit that some of my woodwork joints left a bit to be desired. They had 'toothache' as we used to say and needed a dab of glue to firm them up.

I was working away at my bench, with Frank Beech on one side and 'Flowery' on the other, when Mr Fern spoke.

"Haines".

"Half a mo sir....I'm nearly finished".

Half a dozen rubs with some sandpaper and the job looked okay. I then walked around the bench and stood in front of the Master.

"Yes sir".

Mr Fern hit me so hard across the side of my face that I all but went to the ground. His face was a mask of anger.

"Don't you ever say half a mo to me boy", he said through gritted teeth.

I blinked back tears from shock as much as anything and just stood there. The whole class watched in total silence.

"Now get back to your bench".

I skulked back, still totally unaware of what he had wanted or what I'd done to deserve what I got. The lesson eventually came to an end and I was glad to get out from there; woodwork never gave me the same level of enjoyment again.

When I got home the hay-making was well underway. Jack Barrington was halfway through the baling and Tony and I were allocated the job of putting the bales into piles of four or six to make collecting a bit easier.

In the distance we heard the sound of a motor; it was our Dave, he had turned up to give a hand with getting in the bales. The little Austin Ruby spluttered to a standstill, the door swung open and out he jumped.

"I should have thought you'd have already got that bit in by now", he said, smiling broadly at Tony and winking.

"You bloody wish we had you mean", replied Harold, whose sweaty brow was by then covered in hayseeds.

With all of us working together, we got the last bale in an hour later and the men sat down to enjoy a smoke. It was while they were puffing away that Dave said he'd better mention a little incident; he said that it might just appear in one of the local papers some time in the near future. Harold took a deep puff on his cigarette and wondered what scrape we were going to hear about; Tony and I turned and gave him our undivided attention.

Dave lit his pipe and sent up plumes of thick smoke as a prelude to his story.

"Well", he said, "it was like this....."

The story began several days earlier with Police Constable Frank Hawkins pushing his bike up the Plump Hill. He rarely seemed to pedal the thing as he either pushed it up hills or free-wheeled back down them. PC Hawkins had been the village 'bobby' in Mitcheldean for a number of years and was well known to everyone. He parked his bike at the end of Glencoe Lane, took off his helmet and wiped his brow with a whitish handkerchief. He was a hefty chap who was going a bit thin on top; the trip had taken a fair bit out of him as it had been uphill all the way.

The old wrought iron garden gates creaked as he pushed them open and made his way along a veranda that led to Dave's front door. He knocked loudly on one of the small clear glass panels and stepped back to look down at the garden way below him. It was nicely up together with rows of peas and kidney beans, and green stuff in abundance.

Inside the house, Dave's wife, Pat, had just settled down their toddler daughter Sue, and was a bit annoyed at the heavy handed knocking at the door. The Constable could see that she was far from happy as she walked up the hallway undoing her pinafore as she did so. Pat was a very attractive girl with her long fair hair and slim figure; however Frank Hawkins had weightier matters on his mind.

"Morning my dear".

"Oh hello Frank ....how are you?"

Pat's earlier frown had turned into a warm smile when she saw Frank Hawkins, a man whom she had known for ages and liked a lot.

"Pat I've just come to offer to go to court with Dave and show some support to the boy".

"What are you talking about Frank?"

At this point he realised that Dave had not yet told Pat of his latest escapade. Frank stuttered as he tried to think how best to deal with the situation. In the end he explained that Dave had been caught poaching somewhere up on the Cotswolds; he didn't expand upon it, just re-emphasised that he was willing to go to court with him and show his support. Frank then put his helmet back on, adjusted the chin-strap and made his way to the gate.

"Don't you worry my dear, it'll be alright", he said encouragingly as he retrieved his bike and prepared for the speedy descent back down to the centre of Mitcheldean.

Pat had a thoughtful expression on her face as she closed the front door and went back inside to check on Sue. Having done that, she carried on with the housework and meal preparation which took her right up to teatime.

Dave strolled in at his usual time and tossed his sandwich box and flask onto the chair.

"I could murder a nice cup of tea", he said.

Pat filled the kettle and switched it on. She splashed some milk into two cups and

Lightly Poached

• *Dave tries to bag a pheasant.*

turned to Dave.

"Any news today?"

"No.....nothing worth mentioning".

"Nothing at all you want to tell me?"

Dave shook his head; "'ent that tea ready yet?"

"It's just that Frank Hawkins called by this morning to say that he would be happy to go and support you in court".

"Oh that....I was going to tell you all about it".

"I think you better had my boy.......starting now".

Dave took out his pipe, charged it with tobacco and lit it with great care. Pat poured the tea and waited patiently; this was not Dave's first scrape with authority.

"Well......I was just driving along a little road up past the 'Highwayman Inn'..."

Pat thought what a long way round it was to go up over the Cotswolds when going to work at Mitcheldean, but she held her tongue. Dave explained that he had parked his car in a little side lane with a leafy hedge either side. He put a handful of 410 cartridges in his pocket and retrieved the shotgun pistol from under the car seat. The car was then locked and the door handle twisted several times to make sure it was secure

Dave edged his way along behind a dry-stone wall. On the other side were half a dozen pheasants, all pecking away at some morsels revealed by the recent rain. He cocked both hammers and peered cautiously over the wall with the pistol raised in front of him. The birds were quite close together so he took aim at the nearest one, fired then immediately fired again at the next one to it. The discharge of the gun was very loud and could easily be heard a mile away. He looked around furtively, trying to spot any human movement in the distance. It seemed all clear and so he vaulted over the wall, picked up the two pheasants and stuffed them down inside the lining of his jacket.

Not content with two birds, Dave pressed on with gun in hand. He walked across two fields, keeping close to walls and copses to reduce the risk of being seen. Eventually he crept up on some more pheasants and managed to bag one of them. Even then he pushed his luck to the limit and kept trying for more. He would have been much wiser sticking with the first two and clearing off as fast as he could. He had in fact been heard by people on the estate and then spotted from a distance. They yelled at him to get from there. It was advice he took readily; he ran as fast as he could with the handicap of a jacket full of pheasants and trying to conceal a shotgun pistol at the same time.

It took him nearly ten minutes to get back to the gateway near his car. He was gasping for breath but at same time exhilarated by his law-breaking exploits. There was no-one near the car so he unlocked it quickly and threw the pheasants and the pistol on the floor behind the driver's seat. An old blanket was then spread over them to conceal the evidence.

He felt rather pleased with himself, thinking he had got away with it again. If he hadn't been so confident, he would have hidden the birds and the gun and returned later.

The Austin burst into life at the first attempt; Dave engaged reverse and looked over his shoulder. He was staggered to see a Landrover pull up and block his exit. A man leapt out; he was wearing a felt Trilby hat, a check jacket and a furious expression on his reddened face. He was also waving a stick..

Dave was not the sort to panic, nor was he the sort to give up easily; he scraped the car into first gear and headed on down the little track. The car bumped and lurched along until the angry figure in the rear mirror finally disappeared. He had no idea where he would come out, he just kept going. Ahead of him there seemed to be an exit onto another small road. Dave smiled to himself as he thought of the chap behind him, probably still cursing.

Just then a tractor and trailer pulled across the end of the track and blocked it completely. The smile vanished as he realised he was trapped. He flicked the door handles to lock them from the inside and just sat there. The gamekeeper chap caught up from behind and joined forces with the other chap who looked like a farm-worker. He tapped on the car window with his stick, then tried the handle.

"Come on then.....open up....there's no way out of here now".

The gamekeeper was correct, there was no way out but Dave still didn't move or unlock the car. The men outside were becoming angrier and very frustrated with the crazy situation they were trying to deal with. From a distance they had seen this man shooting and were convinced there were pheasants concealed inside.

"We can wait here all day.....it would be better on you to make a clean breast of it here and now".

Somewhere in Dave's questionable logic was the belief that if they found no birds or gun, then they couldn't prosecute. The one-sided conversation went on for an incredible two hours! Dave never replied to any questions or even moved. It must have been quite unreal; no-one who is innocent just sits in a car in silence for two hours. The farm-worker obviously had more important things to do than stand around in a lane waiting for a poacher to make a confession. He started arguing with the gamekeeper. Soon after he decided he had been there long enough; he took off down the lane and started his tractor, leaving the exasperated gamekeeper still trying vainly to get Dave to own up.

It was to no avail, he turned the ignition key, started the car and pulled off. The incandescent chap waved him goodbye....with his fist!

"When did all this happen?" asked Pat.

"Oh about a week ago", replied Dave, "that day I was a bit late getting home".

"Didn't it occur to you they had your car number?"

"Yea....but if they didn't find any birds…how can they summons me?"

"Well Frank Hawkins wasn't up this morning just for his health was he?"

"Oh they'll just have me for discharging a firearm in a public place I expect", said Dave, obviously not too worried about the whole episode. "But there is one other thing".

"What else could there be", sighed Pat.

"Well you know that nice new watch you bought me".

She had a resigned look on her face as she turned to Dave and nodded.

"The face is smashed".

"How did that happen?"

"I used my forearm to steady the pistol; the damn thing kicked and the barrel came down on the face and hands".

Pat looked out of the window and counted up to ten.

Harold had listened to the tale without interrupting. He then shuffled around on the bale of hay he was using for a seat and looked at Dave.

"Who dost thee think thee bist?.....Dick bloody Turpin?"

We all laughed until the tears ran down our cheeks. We didn't bother to mention it to Mother, it would only have started her off again.

Frank Hawkins did accompany Dave to court on the required date and, incredible as it might seem, he was quite right with his prediction. When the court appearance came to an end, he was only done for discharging a firearm despite his crazy antics in a Cotswold country lane!

Lightly Poached

Chapter Seven
Late 1957

Starting back to school after the Summer holidays soon jolted us out of our carefree attitude; Messrs Aveston, Allott and Jones saw to that. Latin, History and French with them were never going to be a barrel of laughs. Olas Jones, who took us for French, was a bit of a culture shock after Miss Birde-Jones who had taken us for the first year. She would enter a noisy classroom and say, "don't worry about me, I'm just the one who hands out extra work".

Olas was a different kettle of fish altogether, he was a small chap, quite elderly and as bald as a coot. He wore circular rimmed glasses through which he peered like a mole, giving us the impression of having very bad sight indeed. He would stand up at the blackboard and write with his nose about two inches from it. The result was that his gown was invariably covered in chalk dust. We would flick pellets at each other when we thought his attention was elsewhere.

"Stop that..boy", he would shout without turning around, "I can see your reflection in my glasses so don't try it again".

All would go very quiet. We weren't sure whether or not it was just good guesswork, or if his eyesight was so poor that he really could focus on his own lenses. Either way it was prudent to keep still and avoid a blackboard rubber flying in your direction!

By the time you had negotiated the date in Latin and avoided flying objects in French, you were ready for some lunch. It was served in two sittings. Half the school went to 'first lunch' and the other half went to 'second lunch'. Everyone had the same one hour break, so the only difference was whether the 'play' time was before or after eating.

The canteen was a long narrow building, vaguely reminiscent of the old WW1 wards up at Gloucester Hospital. It was located alongside the girls' yard and was joined onto the end of Mr Fern's Woodwork and Metalwork rooms. The canteen was the domain of Mrs Perrett, a small but indomitable lady who ran the kitchen area like an army camp.

Inside were two rows of tables set out like the rungs on two long ladders. The one end of each table was pushed up against the nearest wall and there was a wide gangway down the middle. Boys were segregated in the one row and girls in the other. Each table seated eight pupils; they sat on hard wooden forms that gave little or no concession to comfort. The pupils who happened to be sat in the two 'outside' positions were the 'food monitors' for the day.

The changeover from first to second lunch was a risky business for innocent bystanders. That was because when the time approached for second lunch, the boys all lined up at the edge of the girls' yard. They were kept in check by prefects and the whole thing resembled getting ready for the start of the Grand National! When the bell eventually sounded to signal the 'off', prefects and girls flattened themselves against the railings to avoid being mown down by the careering mob.

On reaching the canteen door the boys were again restrained by another prefect and forced into a long, orderly queue. The pupils towards the back stood in a calm, orderly manner; at the front however, it was rather different. The boys in positions seven and eight started to jostle; unless they could haul some poor unsuspecting 'first formers' into the line, they would end up as food monitors and have to wait table on six others. It was not a pretty sight. Gradually the line sorted itself out; six hulking bruisers were followed by two 'slaves', then six more bruisers and so on.

When the prefect was given the nod by the staff, he or she would jump smartly to one side and let the jostling line of boys into the canteen. A firm grip was kept on the 'slaves' at this time to prevent them making a run for it. We were always made to start filling tables from the end nearest the serving hatch. The first six bruisers would take their seats and the two unfortunate 'slaves' were plonked on the end. This went on for a while until there were no more designated 'slaves', and at this point a slight problem would occur. The remaining tables would end up with only six boys on them, the supposed end two just hopped onto the next empty table to avoid being food monitors.

Chaos then ensued. Attempts to extract the culprits became complicated and the tail-end of the queue all ended up as waiters. It wouldn't perhaps have been so bad if everyone just had the standard meal; but they didn't.

"No gravy for me", yelled Antony Meek, "it's 'orrible".

"No cabbage for me", added Frankie Beech.

"No cabbage or gravy for me", chipped in Benny.

What a nightmare! Dave Holder, 'Flowery' and 'Younger' were lucky, they went home for lunch and so missed our daily treat. Talking of treats, my worst memory of a school meal was cheese flan, beetroot and mash. The mash always had big lumps of boiled potato in it, the flan was a bit like eating a discus and I didn't like beetroot at all. And, if we were really unlucky enough to have 'frog's spawn' semolina on the same day, it was just too much to bear.

I was always really glad to get home on such days and have something to eat; that itself indicated the level of my desperation as Mother was not a great cook herself. Her porridge was still baffling the finest scientists in the land, and her bread pudding was really something to behold!

Anyway, I was eating my tea one day together with Harold and Tony as they were taking a quick break before starting the milking. Harold was browsing through the local paper.

"That was a bad job in Minsterworth", he said looking over the top of the *'Mercury'*.

"What was that then?", enquired Mother as she topped up the mugs of tea.

"Well apparently this lorry ploughed into a flock of sheep".

Mother shuddered as Harold went on to explain that a lorry driver had swerved violently to avoid another vehicle that had lost control, and then careered up onto a wide grassy verge. Unfortunately there was a large flock of sheep grazing there at the time and the lorry just ploughed into them. Seven were killed outright, seven others were put down as soon as the RSPCA man arrived and a further fourteen were pinned under the vehicle. It must have been a ghastly sight.

"Oh....that was dreadful", murmured Mother.

"Somebody will be in for it over that", added Tony.

I pushed my tea to the back of the plate and placed my knife and fork neatly on the top; I didn't really fancy much to eat after hearing the details of that awful accident. Mother looked around the gloomy faces in the room.

"I've got something to show you all", she said brightly.

She disappeared for just a moment then returned with a large, rolled-up drawing. A couple of mugs and plates were pushed hurriedly to one side and the drawing rolled out on the table.

"What do you think of that then?"

We found ourselves peering at an architect's drawing; it was the design of a bungalow.

"What is it about?" I asked.

"It's our new home", replied Mother, " or at least it will be when it has been built".

There had been some vague discussion about a new house from time to time, but I had no idea that my parents had pressed on with it. I had somehow assumed that we would always live in the rambling old farmhouse with draughts and mice for company. However, Mother and Father had talked it over and decided that, as the farm was doing well as a business, then a new house was the next priority. The plan was to build it on the brow of the hill just up from the main barn, by the side of the small track that led down to the Pike House and the George Lane.

The plans were submitted to the local authorities and eventually approved; the next step was to select a builder. Mother was the business brain in the family and Father kept well out of the selection process. Eventually, a local builder was chosen; his name was Frank 'Doody' Middlecote and he lived near the Cross in Littledean. 'Doody' was in partnership with Sid Etheridge, a giant of a man from Cinderford. 'Doody's' brother George and labourer Trevor Wiggle made up the rest of the workforce. The team had been chosen because they enjoyed an excellent reputation locally and had put up some fine houses.

'Doody' and George were quite different physically; 'Doody' was of medium height but was quite slim, almost gaunt in appearance, while George was short and stocky, built a bit like a brick shed. In fact 'Doody' had been a very useful footballer with Cinderford Town a few years earlier and was renowned for his goal scoring. He would head the old-style leather ball so hard it would fly into the net like a cannonball. However, by late 1957 he was concentrating on building up the business. The brothers were extremely friendly, as was Trevor, the fourth and final member of the team. Trevor and Sid were very powerfully built men, both had hands like dinner plates and would not have looked out of place in the wrestling ring. Trevor's short back and sides haircut looked like Ivor Dobbs' handiwork to me, but on a building site it was probably better to be cool than stylish.

The team soon made a start with digging the footings. Trevor and George did the majority of that heavy work and shed a lot of sweat while doing it. On weekends and sometimes after school, I liked to spend my time with the builders. They seemed quite indulgent and didn't mind having me around the site, as long as I kept out of the way and didn't knock dirt back down into the trenches.

They worked really hard and thoroughly deserved their occasional break. It was during one of these breaks that I discovered the delights of cold tea. Each man brought an old pop bottle-full in his bag. It had been made hours earlier with the milk and sugar already added. It was ready to drink straight from the bottle. I must admit that it looked and sounded horrible; it must have shown on my face.

"Do you want a drop?", asked Trevor. "It'll put some hairs on yer chest".

He undid the stopper and passed the bottle to me. It would have been very rude to have declined his generous offer to share his drink. I took a swig and, to my complete surprise, I found it was quite refreshing and tasted rather good. My expression must have changed somewhat. Trevor nodded as he took the bottle back.

"Told you it was alright didn't I?" he said in between swigs, "if you don't try these things then you'll never find out".

It was very good advice, I thought I'd try to remember it whenever possible.

Within a few weeks the footings were in. There was no 'Readymix' lorry or anything like that, just Trevor on the mixer and George on the barrow. 'Doody' and Sid did the finishing work and levelled it all out. Several courses of rustic bricks were then laid and that brought the building up to the damp course level.

Trevor turned off the mixer one morning and it was a merciful relief when it stopped. There had been four or five half-bricks and a bucket of water banging and swishing around inside it for a quarter of an hour or more. He tilted the mixer and the

• *A pair of wagtails enjoy a puddle.*

bricks tumbled out to reveal a clean and shiny interior once more. There were large puddles of water nearby from a hose-pipe that had been left on, these had attracted the attention of a pair of pied wagtails who flew to a safe distance as Trevor splashed by. By then it was time for a break and some concrete blocks were hastily organised as seats.

"Have they got them sods yet who dug up the trees at Speech House?" asked Sid.

He was referring to the trees planted some months earlier by the Queen and the Duke of Edinburgh, and which had been vandalised. There was a real hue and cry over it.

"Was it you and your Dave?" asked 'Doody' with smile all over his face.

"No it wasn't", I blurted, "we haven't been near the place".

"Just as well there weren't any pheasants roosting in them trees", said George, "or else we might not believe you".

The men sniggered among themselves, it set the pattern of conversation for the next few months.

The bungalow was to be built using 'Forest' stone and the next stage was to fetch a decent quantity from the Stone Works at Parkend. 'Doody' had recently acquired a small, fairly new lorry; it had probably been purchased on the back of securing Mother's contract. It was a sombre grey in colour and was open backed with hinged sides and tailgate. The vehicle was ideal for picking up loads of sand, gravel or stone.

'Doody' was always quite willing to take me along and I enjoyed being with the

• *The Stone Works at Parkend.*

'men'. There was a long bench seat in the cab and, with something of a squeeze, we all just about fitted in. Legs sometimes got in the way of gear changes but, as 'Doody' rarely seemed to get out of second gear anyway, it wasn't too much of a problem.

Pulling out onto the main road by the George Hotel was always a bit tricky; you were on a steep hill and it was difficult to see the oncoming traffic. He stalled the engine and cursed loudly, much to the amusement of 'Tuppy' Wynn and Gerald Newman who were loitering near the bus-stop. They were grinning and pointing at me so I gave them a "V" sign as we finally got going again.

"Mates of yours?" enquired George casually.

"Them two beggars haven't got any mates", I replied, "if I had my way I'd set Mrs Baldwin's dog on 'em!"

The lorry moved slowly up past the Guest House Hotel. 'Doody' was such a careful driver that a push-bike could have overtaken us as we crept up the New Road towards Cinderford. It was a great relief to make it to the top of Littledean Hill and then get over the brow by the Mount Pleasant Inn. The going was then much easier; we pressed on towards Speech House and on down the hill to the Cannop cross-roads. We turned left and went for another 100 yards before pulling into the old charcoal works. There wasn't much in there besides a large weigh-bridge and a long brick building. 'Doody' pulled up and the rest of us jumped out. He then inched the lorry onto the weigh-bridge.

"Why have we got out?", I asked, "there 'ent anything here".

"we've got to weigh the lorry old butt", replied George, "then weigh it again when we've loaded the stone".

I didn't ask any more questions; 'Doody' completed the weighing and got some paperwork from inside the shed with the tare weight printed on it. That was the signal for us to pile back on board and get moving once more. It felt almost like a holiday; there I was out joking with the workmen as we cruised along with beautiful trees either side of the road and a huge lake over on our left. We motored on for about another mile before we finally pulled up at the gate of the Stone Works. It was a rambling looking place; there was one huge shed in the centre and a number of smaller ones to the one side. They were all built with corrugated zinc sheets, most of which were a deep, rusty-brown in colour, and a number were missing altogether. The area outside the sheds was strewn with large boulders weighing several tons each as well as piles of much smaller stones.

I followed the others into the big shed where the noise was deafening. There were a series of huge circular saws cutting into gigantic slabs of grey stone. Jets of water were directed onto the cutting areas to cool the blades; there it mixed with the stone-dust to form a creamy fluid which was then piped away. I had never considered that you could actually use a saw on hard rock because, if I had tried it at home, I'd have got a clip around the ear for my trouble. It seemed to me that the cutting edge would be blunted immediately, but I was wrong and had learned something new.

'Doody' had some sort of conversation with the boss at the Stone Works; it must have been difficult above the screeching of the saws. There was a lot of pointing and cupping of hands to ears before they finally sorted out the next step. I followed the men back outside and down the yard to a huge pile of sawn stone.

The pile was made up of mainly grey stone and was in several different sizes. The smallest was the size of a brick and the largest was like a concrete block. The stone had been sawn on three faces only; they would become the top, bottom and front of the block. The sides and back of the pieces were just a quarried finish.

'Doody' went to the cab of his lorry and retrieved a bolster chisel and a lump hammer. He then selected a piece of stone from the pile and took it to one side. There he trimmed the left and right edges so expertly it looked as if they had also been sawn. I could then see what it was all about; they were buying partly finished stone blocks and then using hand tools to customise them on site ready for the building work. 'Doody' was well pleased with how cleanly the stone could be hand cut and nodded to George and Trevor.

"Load her up boys".

I watched them sift and select the most suitable pieces, always taking care to keep to the required ratio of small, medium and large sizes. The back of the lorry started to fill up and the suspension went lower and lower until the tyres seemed to be almost flat. During that time I had got a good idea of what we were looking for and was able to pitch in and help a little.

When 'Doody' judged that his little lorry could take no more, we stopped the loading and edged gingerly out onto the road before heading back to the weigh-bridge. A chap from the Stone Works came with us to verify the weight. We jumped out once more and stood clear as the hand on the giant dial swung right round with the additional tonnage of stone.

"Why didn't we stay on the lorry when we first weighed it?" I asked George.

"'Cos the weight of the lorry would be wrong of course".

"Ay I know....but if we stayed on when the lorry was empty and got off when it was full, we could got some stone for nothing couldn't we?"

"I reckon thou'st might go a long way.....if thou dosn't end up inside", added Trevor, nodding and winking to George as he spoke.

When the paperwork was sorted, we headed back up the hill towards the Speech House Hotel. If I thought we were slow going over to the Stone Works then you can imagine the speed we were travelling back under full load. Trevor obviously felt some conversation was needed and cleared his throat.

"Have you been back to the Pictures since the fire?"

"No....I haven't been inside a Picture House in years", replied George, keeping his left hand free to get at the door handle if needed.

'Doody' was by then in first gear and there was some doubt in my mind that we were going to get up the hill. I wondered if we had put too much stone on board and, as I was wedged in between Trevor and George, wondered if baling out was going to be difficult. Time seemed to have stood still for ages before 'Doody' eventually spoke.

"They reckon it looks quite nice now".

"What does?" asked Trevor.

"The bloody Picture House of course", snapped 'Doody', "what the hell did you think I was on about?"

It seemed the driver was feeling the strain, maybe he was also worried that the lorry was overloaded. There was no more discussion on the refurbishment of Cinderford Picture House during the rest of the journey home. We turned into the George Lane where 'Tuppy' Wynn and Gerald Newman were still loitering. They recognised the lorry and immediately gave me two-handed 'V' signs until the lorry went out of sight.

It was first gear all the way up the track from the Pike House to the building site. 'Doody' backed the lorry into position for unloading and jumped down out of the cab, no doubt relieved to have successfully managed the first of what would be many trips. George opened the passenger door and stepped down and stretched. I was right behind him, glad to get back in one piece.

"We'll have us a break before starting the unloading", said 'Doody' briskly.

Perhaps the lure of a bottle of cold tea was too much for George. Anyway, without thinking, he slammed the lorry door behind him. There was an agonised scream from inside the cab. Trevor was still in the process of getting out and was holding the door-frame when George had slammed the door.

"Bloody hell Trev.....be you alright?" asked a very shaken and apologetic George.

Trevor struggled out of the cab and leaned against the side of the lorry with his injured hand held tightly under his armpit.

"Sorry Trev old butt.....I just didn't see you".

George was really upset, he thought he had smashed poor Trevor's fingers.

"Let's have a look", said 'Doody', who had by then run back to see what the problem was.

He slowly pulled his hand out from under his other arm and held it out. His face was screwed up in pain and you could see why. The edge of the door had cut right in to the bone, all along the line of his knuckles.

"Can you bend your fingers at all Trev?, asked George.

He held out his huge, damaged hand; the fingers were trembling as he tried to flex them. The tips moved only a half inch or so and he winced with the pain.

"Do you want to go up the Dilke Hospital?" asked Sid, who had just returned from another site.

Trevor shook his head, "no I'll be alright in a minute".

They took a bit longer break than usual that day and, by the end of it, Trevor could flex his fingers. He was as tough as old boots; he just wrapped his not-too-clean handkerchief around the knuckles and carried on working. George was mightily relieved I can tell you.

The next few months flew by as the bungalow started to take shape. They did virtually all the work themselves; the only exception I could remember was the windows. They were a large sash design and made by 'Willow' Fox, a skilled specialist from the bottom of Cinderford. He was a silver haired, well-built man who knew his business. And, apart from the fact he could talk the hind leg off a donkey, the work was first class.

Tony and Harold found it hilarious on the days 'Doody' and George had an argument. They would get very angry with each other and their voices would be raised higher and higher until flash-point was reached. That was the signal to Trevor and Sid to keep well out of the way. The brothers would not exchange another word for the rest of the day. 'Doody' would then turn up the following morning with just Trevor in the lorry; George was made to walk to work! It could go on for days!

We had a lot of laughs during those months. I learned some new swear words and rude jokes. It was a very enjoyable time indeed.

Chapter Eight
Late Winter and Spring 1958

There had been a number of snow showers during January. It had been a difficult time for both man and beast. The foxes up in the Grove would make their howling noises late at night; sometimes it was hard to tell the difference between their cries and those of over-excited children. It got worse in February; there was even more snow and then temperatures plummeted, resulting in blizzard conditions. The road from Littledean to Cinderford was very steep and had not been gritted. The full extent of the road chaos could be seen more clearly at first light. Cars and lorries had been abandoned all the way up the hill. A large lorry had ploughed into a number of cars up on 'Sawney's Lookout'. No-one had been killed, mercifully, and the lorry driver was lucky not to have careered through a fence and down the steep bank into some cottages.

Within a few days a good thaw had set in. The snow and ice disappeared quickly and the damaged vehicles were towed away for repairs. Some sort of normality then returned and the builders were grateful to be able to press on with the interior of the bungalow.

Harold had walked to work several times when there had been heavy snow on the roads but, by mid February, he was using the battered Land Rover again. He had parked it early one morning and had gone to the cowsheds and switched on the lights. He screwed up his eyes at the sudden brightness before gathering up some dry sticks. A couple of crinkled pages from the *'Mercury'* were then pressed down into the old, perforated bucket, and the sticks arranged over them.

Bob hovered outside the cowshed. He was already wet through but never seemed to feel the cold or discomfort of wet fur. When Harold came back out he started wagging his tail. The dog was by then seven years-old, middle-aged in canine terms, but he seemed as playful as ever. He barked with impatience as Harold struggled to unlatch the gate leading down to the Orchard. As soon as it was opened, he raced ahead through the thick red mud until he was only just able to see his master through the gloom. He turned, walked back a few paces until he see Harold clearly once more, then bounded

• *Bob always tried to nip the cow's ankles.*

on again. This routine was repeated over and over again as the pair of them squelched their way down through the Orchard to Apple Meadow.

When they reached the main pasture, Harold shouted to the cattle, slapping his stick against the side of his wellington at the same time.

"Come on then....come on then".

The animals turned immediately and headed towards the gateway near to where he was stood. There was the occasional isolated lowing that sounded like a protest at being made to walk to the cowshed for milking yet again. Each time one of the cows walked through the gateway, Bob sneaked out and tried to nip her ankles. It was a habit that resulted in the dog getting plastered with even more mud but, if he was caught with a kick, it cured him for a couple of mornings at least.

Ten minutes later and they were all back inside the two cowsheds. The animals were all latched in their yokes and busy scoffing a cow-cake breakfast. In the corner, just a safe distance from some meal sacks, the brazier had now been lit. Tony had joined Harold by then and they both rubbed their hands and warmed them in front of the crackling sticks. Bob eased his way in through the door and crept as close as he could to the 'bucket of fire'.

After an initial warm, both men pressed on with the milking, leaving the dog to enjoy the final flickering flames. He would doze off, steaming away silently beside the hot embers.

The milking took about one and a half hours. By the time they had finished, it was completely light. The cattle were let back out into the Orchard to make their own way to Apple Meadow and seek out what grazing there was. Bob, now slightly scorched on one side, accompanied the men down to the farmhouse for a well earned breakfast.

I was already sat at the table when I heard their voices outside; there was the familiar sound of wellington boots being stamped on the step to remove excess mud before removal out in the porch.

"You stay there boy", said Harold to the unfortunate dog who was still far too muddy to be allowed inside. Bob looked unhappy about it and made a sort of whispered whining noise as the door was latched.

Mother ladled out three bowls of porridge. It looked awful as usual. It might not have been quite so bad if she had made it immediately before serving it, but she didn't. For some reason she made it maybe half an hour earlier and left it to simmer until we were all assembled. By that time the porridge was no longer porridge at all; it had changed state. It was then a thick grey stodge. We all stared at it for a moment.

"Get it down you, it'll stick to your ribs and keep you warm", she said.

Three spoons clattered three bowls simultaneously. Harold seemed to be able to devour the stuff somehow and even Tony could eventually finish it. I just couldn't. Even when I coated the top with several spoonfuls of sugar, I could only manage a little of it.

"I hear Tim is leaving East Dean", said Tony between mouthfuls.

"Yea....the new headmaster is a bloke named Daffurn", I replied.

I had seen Mr Daffurn just once, it was probably during the interview process as Tim was still in charge at the time. Anyway, everybody reckoned he was the bloke who was going to be the new headmaster. My initial impression was of a rather tall, upright and stern looking man with short, slightly greying hair and a matching coloured moustache. I wondered what East Dean veterans like Messrs Aveston, Allott and Jones would make of their new boss; we would all find out soon that was for sure.

After the breakfast things were cleared, I set off for school and the men went back to work. They had spent part of the previous day fetching two loads of slabbing from Joiners sawmills at Soudley. Their Works was at the floodgate end of the nearby pond, the spot where our Dave had learned to dive many years before. It was also an area that Harold knew quite well. He had been the postman down there for a spell in the late 40's and, as a result, got the off-cut timber on the cheap.

Slabbing was the rough outside skims taken off tree-trunks in the sawmill and it came in a variety of lengths. Most of it was cut up into blocks to be used as fuel and the few half decent pieces were stored to one side.

Tony went into the tractor shed and unhooked a small bow-saw off a nail driven into one of the beams. He emerged seconds later and leaned it against an old, home-made 'sawing horse'. The horse was really just a couple of 'X' shaped end frames held three feet apart and braced with several cross poles, each nailed securely in place. It enabled the sawyer to hold small boughs, poles or stakes quite firmly while cutting then to length or into blocks.

He selected a couple of six foot lengths of slabbing, pieces which resembled a decent plank of wood and had only a small amount of bark on the one side. Tony sawed approximately 18 inches off one end of the first piece then, using it as a master, cut the second piece to exactly the same length. With this completed, he placed the two longer pieces down on the ground and arranged them in an upside down 'V' shape. Another trip was made to the tractor shed, that time he returned with a hammer and a handful of three inch nails. These were driven in along the length of the timber to secure the two pieces together. Tony then turned the construction over and nailed the short lengths to either end. The finished article was a feeding trough for the hens. He was rather pleased with the result and took it over and placed it just outside the coop. All the poultry on the farm were free range and therefore robust feeding troughs were always required, ones that were cheap to produce and easily replaced when they rotted. Tony was still admiring his handiwork when Mother came by; she was about to collect the eggs.

"It's no good just looking at it my boy, we need another three of those".

"Jesus wept Mother", he replied in exasperation, "I've only just this second put the damn thing down there".

Mother swept on by leaving Tony to gnash his teeth. She lifted the little door-flaps on the nest-boxes, then took out the eggs and placed them carefully into a small, straw-lined metal bowl. In each of the nest-box compartments was a single china egg which was left to remind the hens where to lay. Without them some hens would start to lay on the floor of the coop, or even worse, out in the barn or a nearby hedgerow. It was not that rare for a hen to accumulate an undetected clutch of eggs out in some undergrowth, go broody and hatch them without the fox taking her, then return with a dozen or so very young chicks.

Sometimes one of the hens would go broody and refuse to shift off the eggs in the nest-box, thereby forcing other hens to lay elsewhere. It was vital on those occasions to collect the eggs on a daily basis to prevent them being spoiled as far as eating was concerned. Any broody hens would be placed in a darkened crate for a couple of days and that usually cured their hatching instincts.

Mother completed the egg collection while Tony made another trough and Harold sawed up blocks. By mid morning there was a sizeable pile of sawdust on the grass beside the horse.

"Ready for a blow?" enquired Harold.

Tony nodded and wiped his hands before getting a packet of cigarettes from his jacket pocket. He put one in his mouth and offered the packet to Harold. They lit up and sat on a bale of straw in the tractor shed. Bob went in as well and, after turning round in three or four circles, plonked himself down and rested his chin on Harold's wellington boot.

"I hear a ewe has had quads down at Blackrock Farm", said Harold.

"Then they got some bottle feeding to look forward to", replied Tony.

Harold just nodded and took a deep puff.

"We'll go and cut some stakes up in Chestnuts before dinner and then mend a few of them gaps up in the Grove this afternoon".

"Ay alright.....it'll make a break from sawing blocks", replied Tony.

"Come on old butt", said Harold as he placed his hand on the dog's head, "let's do a bit more work".

Armed with a bow-saw and a hacker, the men headed along the Common and into the Chestnuts Inclosure. The area had been stripped of all the mature trees a few years earlier and was now covered in a mixture of small broad-leafed and evergreen trees. They weren't interested in the evergreens of course but there were plenty of stakes to be had from the rest. The stakes were only going to be used for repair work, so more or less any straight piece would do, as long as it was about six feet long and strong enough to be hit into the ground with the sledgehammer.

It took them no more than an hour to cut and sharpen 20 stakes. These were carried down to the Inclosure fence and placed surreptitiously in some undergrowth.

"You stay here and keep an eye on 'em", instructed Harold, "and I'll go and fetch the tractor".

Tony looked around nervously to make sure they hadn't been seen. It all seemed quiet and still so he lit up and waited. Harold returned five minutes later. He left the engine running as they hurried to load the stakes into the tractor box. Then Bob suddenly started barking loudly.

"Shut up boy", hissed Harold.

The dog came round to the back of the tractor.

"What's the matter with thee?" asked Tony.

The dog wagged his tail and kept looking towards some undergrowth. A couple of tatty looking sheep emerged seconds later with briars dangling from their wool; it set Bob off again. I think even the dog was on edge!

The tractor was parked up by the farmhouse and the men went in for a well earned rest. The lunch was not very special, Mother had done some rather fatty and salty home-cured bacon with boiled potatoes. However, on a cold day and after a few hours of hard labour, most things seemed to fill a gap. Both Harold and Tony nodded off in their armchairs after the meal. The lunch-break usually lasted until Harold woke up. That was because if Tony woke first, he just closed his eyes again.

By two o' clock they were both on the tractor heading towards the Grove. Bob barked his head off as usual and tried to bite the front tyres as they turned. Harold ignored him and pressed on until he reached the gate into the Lower Grove. Tony hopped off and opened it without difficulty as it was one of our better gates. Bob raced into the field and expended a considerable amount of energy racing backwards and forwards while waiting for the tractor and the men to catch up.

Harold drove as far as he could up the steep bank of the Upper Grove, or Bryants Grove as it was called long ago. He switched off the engine, jumped down and stretched his legs.

There were a number of weak points in the top hedge. Ewes had got out through it a couple of times before and only very temporary repairs had been done each time. Unfortunately for the men, the gaps were in a part of the hedge some 200 yards further up the steep slope. It was where Father had accidentally burned down a wide section of hedge some years earlier while trying to clear gorse bushes. The fence that had been erected hastily at the time was now broken in places and the hedge had not yet re-grown properly. The result was that our ewes got into Hayward's fields and vice versa.

Tony bundled up a dozen stakes and tied them up with baling string. He then heaved them up onto his shoulder and headed off up the hill followed by Harold

•*The Roman Camp viewed from Littledean Hill.*

carrying the tools and a reel of barbed wire. It took them ten minutes to reach the top of the Grove. Tony was exhausted by then and let the bundle of stakes fall to the ground. He had tried to carry too many in one go and certainly knew about it by the time he reached the top hedge. Harold tossed down the reel of wire and slumped down on the bundle of stakes next to Tony. He took out a cigarette and, without speaking, offered the packet to Tony. They lit up and gazed down the valley between Chestnuts Wood and the Roman Camp, and on towards the horseshoe bend in the Severn. Below them they could see virtually all of Greenway Farm; the view of the large fields was very different to the patchwork of small plots worked by tenants a century earlier.

Neither of the men spoke; it had been a steep climb and both were still getting their breath back. Bob was also feeling it a bit. He was sat on his haunches panting furiously, his long pink tongue dangling out of the side of his mouth.

I had been sat with Harold and Tony in more or less the same spot many years earlier. Tony had asked me at the time if I knew why badgers had two short legs on the one side and two longer legs on the other. I didn't know of course and he went on to explain that it was to enable them to walk along the side of a hill.

"Well ...what happens if they want to come back the same way then?" I had asked naively.

"They can't come back......they've got to go right round the other side of the hill to get back where they started from".

I must have looked a bit unconvinced as he looked to Harold for support.

"'Ent that right Harold?"

"Ay that's right.....believe me", said Harold in all seriousness.

I believed that load of old cobblers for years after that...the rotten sods!

When they had all got a second wind and extracted the last few puffs from their cigarettes, they turned to the job in hand. There were several thin patches in the hedge, each with the tell-tale signs of sheeps' wool dangling from the branches. Harold sent Bob to round up several of Hayward's ewes and lambs that had come through from The Odd Marks, the curiously named field on the top side of the Grove.

"Lie down.....lie down", he shouted to the dog as the trespassers hurled themselves through the gaps, enlarging them as they did so.

"Damn things", Harold muttered to himself.

Tony smiled broadly, recalling in his mind the picture of Father accidentally setting fire to the hedge. In fact it was more a case of 'damn matches' than 'damn sheep'.

Harold held a stake while Tony hammered it into the ground with the sledge. Away in the distance, Mother looked across towards the Grove as she fed the chickens. For a moment she watched the quite unreal delay between the sledge hitting the stake and the sound carrying across the valley to where she was stood.

The stakes were spaced about 18 inches apart along the length of the poor sections of hedge. Living branches were bent over and weaved in and out of the stakes. It was not possible to do a proper laying job as there just wasn't enough growth. Harold then nailed three strands of barbed wire in place to strengthen the repair and give the hedge a chance to grow.

Over the next hour they repaired several poor sections; it was not perfect by any means but it was a lot tidier than the alternative of rusty corrugated sheets nailed into place.

"There's some sort of foxes back up here", remarked Tony as he looked at the series of fresh mounds of soil along the butt of the hedge.

"Ay...they're back in numbers that's for sure...if we start to lose any hens then we'll have to get Rover up here".

Rover was Dave's little dog; he was equally as good at sniffing out pheasants above ground as he was fetching out foxes from under ground.

The men collected up the tools and made their way back down over the Grove, leaving the earthy smell of foxes way behind them. When they got back to the farmhouse, another job was being lined up for them.

"We shall be moving next week according to 'Doody'", said Mother as she looked around the old beams in the living room.

I guess she had the same mixed feelings as the rest of us. It was great to be moving into a new home with all mod cons, but it was strange to be leaving the old homestead despite the draughts and mice. We would probably have moved a week earlier only George Middlecote had hit a snag when trying to dig out a hole for the septic tank. It was solid clay and he had to fetch it out by hand; there was no mechanical digger in 'Doody's' organisation, just George and his spade. I can still see him so clearly; he was stripped to the waist and sweating profusely. He would thrust his spade into the clay four times to mark out a square, then lever each chunk out before throwing it up over onto the other red cubes. The problem was of course that there was no chance of putting in soak-away pipes in that sort of ground as the water would have nowhere to go. The upshot was that a 25 yard ditch had to be dug to reach a more suitable soakaway area way on down the proposed new garden. The work was deemed to be outside the contract and so Tony got lumbered with the additional ditch digging task.

When the weekend arrived, Tony was glad when Dave turned up to collect him for a poaching expedition. Rover jumped out of the car and started barking. The little black and tan terrier was excited, he knew he was off shooting and lived for such afternoons.

"Fancy trying over Ledbury way for a change?" asked Dave.

"Ay why not", replied Tony, just glad to see the back of the ditch digging, "whereabouts at Ledbury?"

"We got to pick up my mate from Lydbrook, he reckons we could get some birds over on the Eastnor Estate".

"Who is this bloke?"

"Gerald Nicholson...he's alright", said Dave.

Apparently Gerald worked at Ranks with Dave and they had become friends; a relative of his had worked on the Eastnor Estate at one time and had plenty of stories of pheasants just there for the taking.

Tony put on a heavy raincoat and retrieved his 12 bore from the house. He broke it down into its three parts and placed them carefully in the boot of the car. With a full packet of cigarettes and a handful of bright red Eley cartridges, he was ready to go.

Dave drove down to the outskirts of Lydbrook, not far from the Yew Tree pub. He sounded the horn outside a small cottage perched on the side of a steep bank. Moments later a young, fit looking man appeared in the doorway. He had short, wavy dark hair and looked a bit of a rogue. It was Gerald, the third member of the raiding party.

"Gerald..this is our Tony", said Dave.

He jumped into the back of the car by the side of Rover who looked him over very carefully. The men shook hands over the top of the passenger seat and Gerald placed the sack containing his shotgun between his knees.

"Not a bad day for it", remarked Gerald brightly.

"Yea.. nice and overcast so not too many people about...do you want a fag?" asked Tony.

"Ay...don't mind if I do".

They all lit up and Dave headed the car down through Lydbrook and along by the river.

"'Taffy' Gardiner reckons he know the places where the salmon stay at low tide....we'll have a go at catching some when he says the time is right", said Dave.

'Taffy' was yet another mate. He lived in Ruardean and was a Glosters veteran; he had fought alongside Dave, Royston Mills and several other local lads at the Imjin River battle. They belonged to an exclusive club, they had all endured the long years together in the Yalu River POW camp.

Tony rolled his eyes, drew hard on his cigarette and said nothing; he still vividly remembered 'Taffy's' previous fishing expedition. It had been, according to 'Taffy', a guaranteed method of catching pike. All three of them had spent the best part of three hours catching some small roach to use as live bait. They then spent the rest of the day, nearly five more hours, trying to hook a pike; they hadn't even managed a single bite!

Conversation covered an array of subjects during the next half hour as they neared their destination. They were still a couple of miles from Ledbury when Gerald leaned over between the front seats.

"There's a turning on the right soon, we'll go down it a few hundred yards and park in a little lane down there".

He was spot on; they took the next turning and were able to get the car more or less out of sight in a gateway set well back from the road. The men assembled their shotguns, buttoned up their raincoats and headed off across some fields towards a large wooded area.

"Come on Rover...fetch 'em out", whispered Dave.

The little dog was so excited but now there was no barking, just furious tail wagging. He went up and down the edges of paths and clearings with his nose pressed to the ground. Luckily his sense of smell had not been affected by a vicious squirrel bite a few years earlier. Soon his whole body became strangely energised. His to and fro movements always became more and more agitated as he neared a bird in hiding.

"Get ready", whispered Dave.

Safety catches were released and all three men held their guns in front of them, the barrels pointing slightly upwards, ready to whip the stock to the shoulder in an instant. Just then there was a flapping from the undergrowth. A hen pheasant took off. Dave and Tony both fired before Gerald had even raised his gun. Rover raced to where the bird had fallen and grabbed it by the neck. He struggled several times to pick it up before he finally got a good grip and trotted back to Dave.

"Good boy......good boy..".

He patted and praised the dog and, when he had finally managed to prise the bird away, dropped it down inside the lining of his coat.

"We'll get plenty more and share 'em out afterwards", said Dave as he pressed on to keep up with Rover.

Gerald's speed and accuracy with a shotgun left a lot to be desired, although the other two had bagged three hen birds between them over the next hour. They were very pleased indeed and complimented Gerald on his sound advice regarding the Eastnor estate. It had the effect of making him feel good despite his numerous misses with the gun.

"Might as well head back hadn't we?", said Tony, who still had to do the milking.

"Ay...okey doke", replied Dave, "might as well have another of your fags on the way back".

Tony grimaced; Dave only ever smoked a pipe, except that is, when he was able to scrounge a cigarette off his brother. Nevertheless it had been a good and profitable afternoon. They made their way back towards the car feeling rather pleased with themselves. When they were about 80 yards away, Rover stopped and growled.

"What's the matter boy?" asked Dave.

Just then a small brown and white terrier ran around the front of the car. They stood still and watched for a moment. Soon after another little dog joined it. It was rather strange, there was no-one anywhere to be seen yet two small dogs were running around the car. As they walked closer a man stood up, he had been sitting on a low bank behind the car.

"Quick...hide these birds", hissed Dave as he handed his pheasant to Tony, who then tossed all of them into the undergrowth and pushed them out of sight with his boot.

"Ah gentlemen...I think I have caught you red-handed", said the stranger as the men approached him.

He was wearing a tweed outfit with boots and leather gaiters; he was also quite short, middle-aged and very officious.

"I'm sure that you realise that poaching is illegal, so I'll have your names and addresses before we go any further".

"Look", said Dave, "we've just been shooting squirrels....just out for a bit of fun ...that's all".

"I'm having no truck with the likes of you......I want your names and addresses...now".

Dave bristled visibly and Tony flung himself between him and the gamekeeper. He was terrified that Dave was going to smash the man to the ground. If he had realised the short fuse on the man he was dealing with, the gamekeeper would have been much more careful with his manner.

Tony turned and spoke quietly.

"John Watkins and I live at 13, Willow Way, Monmouth".

It was a well rehearsed false address that he had used many times before.

Dave seemed calmer when he spoke again.

"We haven't done anything wrong....but I'm John Thomas from Coney Hill".

He went on to give the detailed address of 'Sailor' Thomas, his old mate from the Glosters. Gerald got the drift of what was happening and made up some name and address as he went along.

"Well as I said...we haven't done anything wrong so we'll be on our way", said Dave.

"You haven't heard the last of this I can assure you", replied the gamekeeper as he jabbed his forefinger towards Dave's chest.

Gerald and Tony grabbed Dave's arms and dragged him to the car. They put their guns in the back with Gerald, Tony took the wheel and shot up the lane as quickly as he could.

"Do you think he saw you hide the pheasants?" asked Gerald.

"Can't be sure", replied Tony.

He glanced across at Dave; the anger in his face was starting to drain away. Tony thought they were lucky that poaching was the only charge likely to be made.

It was about a week later that PC Brunning called at Dave's house. He was the new man in the village and had recently replaced Frank Hawkins. The trace on the car number had of course led the police straight to Dave. PC Brunning was not particularly keen to get his career off to a bad start and, given the evidence, was looking for a conviction.

There wasn't a lot of point in pleading not guilty in the circumstances, and so all three opted to throw themselves on the mercy of the court.

It was more than a month later when Tony, Dave and Gerald headed back to Ledbury, this time to the magistrates' court.

The gamekeeper, whose name turned out to be Mr Pearce, brought the three hen pheasants into court.

"He must have kept 'em in his freezer", whispered Dave.

The other two defendants thought it wiser to keep quiet and wished that Dave would do the same. All three stood silently in their smart white shirts, ties and suits as Mr Pearce droned on about seeing the men emerge from a wood carrying shotguns, and how he saw them hide something in the undergrowth. He then held up the rather stiff looking birds for the court to see, and continued on to explain how he had retrieved them from where they had been hidden. He said that they had been shot recently and were still warm when he had found them. Finally, he laboured the point that all three had been uncooperative and had given false names and addresses. Holding the pheasants high he pointed out in a rather dismissive manner that the men had said they were just out for a bit of fun, shooting squirrels and pigeons to make a little pocket money.

All three pleaded guilty to unlawfully pursuing game and giving false names and addresses; unlawfully carrying guns without licenses; and killing pheasants on a Sunday. They also came out with the usual contrite words about not realising the seriousness of the offence and apologised for any trouble caused.

The chairman of the court then addressed the defendants.

"There are far too many people wandering about the country with guns and not possessing licenses".

He fined them each £10 with 4s 6d costs; it was a lot of money to them, more than a week's wages in fact.

They left the court together and lit cigarettes as they walked to the car.

"It could have been worse I suppose", said Dave.

"Yea you're right....specially if you'd hit the silly beggar like you wanted to", replied Tony.

They laughed at their own misfortune as they set off back home; they hadn't learned their lesson, and it would happen again as sure as apples were apples!

Chapter Nine
Summer and Autumn 1958

We quickly became used to living in the bungalow. It was named 'Greystones' and was warm and comfortable, although Mother's cooking did not improve significantly on her new Rayburn. Porridge, salty pig joints and ageing poultry still featured regularly.

Out in the fields, the lambs were growing like hops and were as big as the ewes. The twice daily chore of milking was relentless, although Harold always organised the work of the day around it. One of those 'in between' jobs was to improve the drainage at the top end of the Apple Meadow near the barn.

The problem was twofold; firstly, some years earlier the council had run storm drains from the Folders estate down into the adjacent field, and secondly, a natural spring cascaded water down from Fred Grindle's hilly field opposite. This formed a stream which flowed under the George Lane and diagonally across our field.

During the Winter and other periods of sustained rain, the combined result was that the end of Apple Meadow became waterlogged. Then add to that the churning effect of cows' hooves, together with tractor deliveries of Winter food, and soon a quagmire was formed.

It took a lot longer to recover than the rest of the pasture and so Harold had decided to do something about it. His plan was to dig a network of trenches; place soakaway pipes in the bottom of them and direct the excess water down into the stream. The slight natural slope at the top end of Apple Meadow worked in their favour, and meant the ditches didn't need to be very deep. Harold had left the drainage job until early Summer; by then it wasn't too muddy and neither was the ground too hard for digging.

Tony bump started the tractor and then parked it near a huge pile of unglazed soakaway pipes. He left the engine running when he hopped off to help Harold load a couple of dozen of them into the tractor box. Two spades and a dawker were then placed carefully beside the pipes before they set off to Apple Meadow. Bob chanced a broken jaw yet again by messing around in front of the wheels. Why he barked and bit the tyres I didn't know, perhaps he was just excited to be on the move.

Ten minutes later they arrived at the designated work area. Tony parked by the barn, lowered the tractor box and switched off the engine. Bob cocked his leg on a couple of tall thistles and sniffed around his territory.

After some discussion and a lot of pointing, Harold and Tony finally agreed where the trenches should be dug. They removed the turf carefully from a ten yard section and placed it neatly on one side of the intended trench. Having done that they started digging from each end and, if they worked at a similar rate, then they were going to meet in the middle. The trench was taken down two spade lengths and, after an hour, the first section was completed. An erratic line of bright red soil had been piled on the side opposite the turf. A robin had appeared from nowhere and made regular raids for the worms that had been displaced and now wriggled in the loose soil.

Both men were blowing hard and sweating freely. They looked at each other and then, without speaking, jabbed their spades into the dirt mound and sat down with their legs dangling in the trench. It was Harold's turn with the cigarettes and he didn't have to be reminded. They lit up and gazed in the general direction of Littledean.

"I hear they're trying to stop the gypsies from staying at Crump Meadow", said Harold.

"Oh".

"Talking about taking 'em to court apparently".

"Well they'll do pretty well if they get any money out of 'em", replied Tony, "still I suppose our Dan will be pleased....they won't be able to set the dogs on him any more".

They both laughed and recalled my earlier bad luck on the cross-country run.

It took about ten minutes to smoke a cigarette and, unless they were in the middle of a heated debate, that normally dictated the length of their breaks. There were still a few puffs to go when something fell into the trench; it started making a strange squeaking noise.

"What the hell is that?" asked Tony.

Harold looked down and then exclaimed, "well I'll be damned....it's a mole".

It seemed that while the men had been digging away, a spade had cut through and sealed the little creature's underground run. And then, when hunger told it to start searching for more worms, it trundled along its network of tunnels and, unfortunately, pushed its way through the blockage and fell headlong down into the trench.

The sudden daylight must have been terrifying. The poor little thing just scampered up and down in blind terror making pathetic noises. Harold bent down, picked it up and had a close look at it.

"Well I'll be damned", he said again.

Although there were moles in most of the fields, they were never considered to be much of a pest. The molehills were easily cleared and a little underground aeration of the soil did no harm at all. Harold walked over to the hedgerow and placed the little fellow in some long grass, well away from the glare of the daylight.

"You'd better dig yourself a new tunnel old mate", he said as he turned and walked back to rejoin Tony.

Work continued on and off for several weeks until like the mole, the men had completed their network of underground tunnels.

• *The poor mole was suddenly out in the bright sunlight*

It was at this time that we all became rather keen on fishing. I'm sure that Dave's mate 'Taffy' Gardiner was behind it all. Not only did he reckoned he knew where the biggest pike were, he also knew how to net salmon, how to tickle trout and so on. According to him he always had to take a wheelbarrow with him to carry the sheer weight of fish back to his home in Ruardean!

Anyway, by then I had my own fairly cheap two piece glass fibre rod and had been fishing down on the Wye several times with Tony and Dave. We were always able to catch a number of bright silvery chub using a bit of cheese rind as bait.

I had arranged to meet my school pal David Holder one Saturday morning and, just for a change, we were going to try our luck down on the Severn. He turned up right on time, puffing hard and looking fresh-faced and freckled. He was starting to sprout up in the air a bit higher than me and his curly brown mop looked as out of control as usual. I reckoned that except for his freckles he was going to look just like Mr Aveston when he was old and grey!

We had already got a plentiful supply of hooks and weights from Edwards' hardware shop up in Cinderford; however, the next job was to sort out some bait. Armed with two hastily cleaned jam-jars with perforated lids, we headed for the dung-

• *A spot of fishing down at Broadoak.*

heap at the back of the cowshed. The manure there was well rotted and heaving with worms. Just jabbing the fork in and shaking it would reveal dozens of them. It took no more than five minutes to half fill both jars.

The rods were tied to the crossbars of our bikes. The saddlebags were then packed with hooks, lead weights, bait, a knife and a pair of pliers to remove hooks; it also came in very handy for pinching the weights onto the line.

"Where exactly are we off to?" asked David.

"Down to Broadoak", I replied, "not far from the White Hart pub".

"How long will it take?"

"Oh about 20 minutes or so....that's all".

I saw Harold walk into the cowshed and went to let him know where we were going.

"You be careful with the tide down there mind", he warned us. "It turns in minutes....just make sure you stay near the bank...that goes for you as well young Holder".

We both nodded appropriately, grabbed our bikes and set off as quickly as we could. It made no sense to hang around and risk getting lumbered with one of Mother's chores. We kept to a leisurely pace along the George Lane, taking care to avoid the occasional dangling briar. Although it was mainly downhill to the river, it made good sense to conserve energy for the arduous return trip.

Jean Hodges and Dorothy Hart watched us pedal up the little hill by the George Hotel. They giggled and pointed at us as we strained up the last few yards.

"Who is that with Danny Haines?" I heard Jean ask.

"I don't know", replied Dorothy and, looking straight at David, asked, "what's your name then?"

David ran his young eyes over Dorothy's not unattractive features. His mouth was about to open when I said to him, rather tersely, "come on....we don't have time to mess with them".

We free-wheeled on down past the Greyhound with our hair flapping wildly and tears streaming across our cheeks. We soon reached Elton Corner where we stopped for a moment to wipe our eyes and laugh at the thrill of our high speed descent. We then crossed onto the main Gloucester to Lydney road and pedalled for about three quarters of a mile before turning down a little side road on the left. Just as we did so, a train hurtled over a bridge just behind us, clattering the rails on its way to Gloucester

The side road took us past a few houses and then, more importantly for us, to a grassy section of bank that was big enough for two or three people to cast from. Luckily, the tide was in and the water was lapping against the bottom of the small bank. We were to find out on other badly-timed visits that the water was separated from the bank by 30 or 40 yards of thick, squelching mud. Fishing was hopeless on such occasions as we struggled to cast out far enough to even reach the water.

However, conditions that morning were fine; within minutes we had assembled our rods, baited the hooks and cast out. We had both cut short, forked sticks from the nearby hedge; these were then jabbed into the bank and the rods rested on them. All that was then required was for the fish to hurl themselves on the hooks and for us to reel them in as fast as we could. We had visions of being overwhelmed with the sheer size of the catch and unable to transport it all home. We need not have worried! It was almost an hour before either of us had a bite. I managed to land a little flatfish about the size of my hand, and David hooked an eel but managed to lose it.

We just lost track of time; we were still enjoying ourselves as the tide started to go out. Just then David had another good bite, it had to be an eel because of the strong pull on the line.

"Keep it coming in or else it will curl around some rocks and break your line", I warned.

He heaved and reeled as fast as he could and managed to look like someone landing a small whale. He kept good tension on the line and soon it was splashing in the shallows.

"It is an eel", confirmed David as he tugged it up along the mud to the bank.

The trouble was it had by then coiled itself up into a moving, slimy mud-covered ball.

"Get the bleeding hook out then".

I tried to get hold of the eel but it was just impossible. Every time I straightened it out, I then lost my grip and the thing turned up into a knot again.

"What are we going to do?....we can't just stand here".

"There's only one thing for it", I said as I got out my penknife.

I managed to get the sole of my shoe onto one end of the squirming creature while David held the line taut. There was no way we were ever going to get the hook out of the thing, so we had to kill it. The only way to do it was to cut off its head. I did it quickly and cleanly.

"Does your mum cook eels?", I asked as we watched the final few wriggles.

"Not sure", he replied, his eyes fixed on the end of his line with the eel's head still dangling on it.

We both managed to catch a few flatfish before the tide went out too far for us to cast; that was the signal to head back for home. We packed our things neatly into the saddlebags and wheeled our bikes out to the main road. Getting to Elton Corner wasn't too bad, but from there it was a long old pull up to Littledean on a push-bike. We stopped several times for a much needed rest and it took us more than an hour to get to Denton's Corner. It made good sense to us to push our bikes from there, taking the little lane up past Mrs Baldwin's nasty dog and along the Common.

Both of us were absolutely starving by the time we got to the bungalow because, although we had chocolate and Milky Ways with us, you didn't really fancy them very much after you have handled worms, eels and flatfish. Mother did us a plate of chips each but reckoned our fish were too small to cook; it was a bitter disappointment, we had talked about nothing else all the way back.

For David there was yet another hurdle to overcome; it was another three miles for him to cycle home and that included the steep hill up to the Barn. When he did finally get home there was still the weekend homework to be done; there was some awful algebra and an English composition to be tackled. I decided to crack on with the English and crib the maths off Terry Barnard on Monday morning.

Terry was nicknamed 'Noski'; I think Dave Meek came up with the name as an abbreviation for Bronowski, the world renowned Professor of mathematics. 'Noski' had more ability in maths, and most other subjects come to that, than the rest of us put together. And, although he looked like a boffin himself with his out of control curly hair and dark rimmed glasses, he was more at ease with our less talented gang than he was with the 'swots'.

I biked to school on Monday morning and got there just after half past eight. I sat on a bench in the cloakroom, hoping against hope that 'Noski' would not be late. He eventually arrived at twenty to nine and I breathed a huge sigh of relief. Several of us cribbed the maths homework at incredible speed as we had only minutes before the bell sounded. Using ink pens didn't help as it was very difficult not to smudge the work in your haste. I cobbled something down and hoped that Mr Brown, the no-nonsense maths master, would just give me five or six out of ten and not make me stand up in class and give an explanation of how I had done it.

The first lesson was geography with Mr Allen. I knew him slightly before going to East Dean because he lived on the outskirts of Littledean in a beautiful white house named 'Margarets'. He was a pleasant chap, almost friendly by East Dean standards. He had been given the nickname of 'Geogger' because at the time that was what we all called geography. He was in his 40's but looked older because of his gaunt appearance; it was almost as if his parchment-like skin had been pulled tight down over his skull. Room five was his classroom and he had the habit of parking his rather smart black Morris Oxford car right outside the window so he could keep an eye on it all day long.

'Geogger' did that morning what he usually did; he wrote neatly on the board in different coloured chalks and we all copied it down into our exercise books. That particular lesson was about fibres and cloth making in different parts of the world; he talked about jute for making sacking and about a number of other poor quality materials. We had a discussion on 'shoddy' which was made from bits and bobs or the shredded fibre of other fabrics that have already been worn or used before.

It was one of life's terrible coincidences that Antony Worsfold's blazer had worn out only days before and was no longer repairable. He had been sent to school wearing a quite hideous sports jacket. I'm not sure if it was an old one belonging to his dad or his uncle, but whatever way you looked at it, its best days were long past. He had endured a torrid time because of it and, as if that wasn't enough, 'Geogger' was there up at the board talking about 'shoddy', and how the word had become synonymous with poor quality cloth. Mutterings and pointing began at the back of the class.

"What is all that noise about?"

There was no reply and the class went very still. 'Geogger' wasn't happy with that and picked on David Holder.

"Holder...what were you talking about?"

David looked awkward and shuffled on his wooden desk seat.

"Sir...we were just wondering if Worsefold's jacket was 'shoddy' or not".

The boys started sniggering again and 'Geogger' did not like losing control.

"If I hear another squeak out of you boys then you'll all stay behind after school".

We all became very quiet and only a few of us heard David Holder whisper "Shoddy" out the side of his mouth to Antony Worsfold. Poor old Antony, he had to endure the nickname 'Shoddy' for the remaining three years at East Dean!

The second lesson was biology with Mr Selley. He was a serious, quietly spoken and dapper man with slicked-back hair and gold rimmed glasses. According to David Holder he was active in the Civil Defence, although it wasn't easy to visualise it. Sometimes he seemed rather bewildered when the boys played him up in class and there was anarchy when we had any practical work. He had given me a 100 lines the previous week and I was hoping he had forgotten all about it.

The Biology lab was set out just like the Physics and Chemistry labs; it had a number of long workbenches running across the width of the room, and a series of cupboards all the way around the outside. At the back there were shelves stacked with large jars containing the preserved remains of frogs and toads and so on.

"Your lines Haines if you please".

I cursed his good memory and thought fast.

"Sir I did my lines but they got ruined".

"Tell me more Haines...I'm fascinated to know how these lines got ruined".

"Well sir, I was walking to school this morning with the lines in my hand, when a crow swooped down and took them away".

Mr Selley just stared at me blankly so I kept going.

"The crow flew on for a bit and then dropped the lines in a puddle; all the ink was washed off sir".

The boys all guffawed and the girls sniggered as they expected me to be marched in to the headmaster's office. Mr Selley just kept staring and I suddenly thought that I'd pushed my luck a bit too far.

"200 lines by tomorrow morning Haines".

"Yes sir", I replied, relieved that my cheek had not got me into really serious trouble.

When I think back to that incident, I truly believe Mr Selley gave me credit for originality, as an extra 100 lines was a very small price to pay for lasting playground fame.

"Today we are going to dissect some worms", he said.

Several of the girls looked as though they were going to be sick. Mr Selley then lit the Bunsen burner on his workbench at the front of the lab. After that he filled a glass container with water and placed the burner under it. He went on to explain how we were going to use scalpels to nick through the outer skin and pin it back either side. For me the project held no fears; after all I had successfully killed Mrs Sutton's chicken for her, however, for some of the others it was going to be quite an ordeal.

The water in the glass container had come to the boil by then. Mr Selley reached down under his bench and retrieved a jar of live worms. He then took a pair of long-nosed tweezers and carefully picked one up and dropped it into the water. I thought Elizabeth Burnett was going to be sick as she started making awful kecking noises.

"Elizabeth…you can go outside for a moment if you need to", said Mr Selley sympathetically.

"No sir….I'll be alright", she replied, in between more convulsions.

"Sir…why are you doing that?", asked Ruth Kirby, who looked as if she had eaten a lemon.

"For dissection the worms need to be fresh, and this is the quickest and most humane way to kill them".

The girls looked at each other somewhat unconvinced; they would clearly have preferred to start the lesson with worms that were already dead. Meanwhile, Mr Selley organised us into pairs to perform the dissections. I was with David Meek who seemed intent on slicing the worm up like a cucumber.

"Be very careful with the scalpels, they are extremely sharp", warned Mr Selley as he buzzed around the lab pointing here and checking there.

By the end of the lesson nearly everyone had a worm nicely dissected, with the outer skin pinned back and the inner bits revealed. We had to sketch it quickly and then draw it up properly for homework, labelling all the parts that we had revealed. That wasn't going to take long, however the 200 lines would take the rest of the evening, plenty of time to reflect on whether or not to keep my big mouth shut in future!

A couple of days later, Harold decided that we needed to replenish some of the hand tools. The pliers were rather worn, the adjusting spanner had 'toothache', and many of the others were rusted or damaged. He had heard of a place called 'The Wyelands' that sold second hand tools at low cost. It seemed the perfect answer to our needs and so, in the evening, Tony and I jumped in the Land Rover beside Harold.

"Where is this 'Wyelands' place then?", I asked out of curiosity.

"Down the bottom of Catshill….on down from Ruardean".

We chugged our way up to the top of the Barn and the old workhorse seemed almost grateful as we descended down Belle Vue road and on through Cinderford itself. There were no trains about and we were soon through the crossing at Steam Mills and on our way up the Morse road.

"Don't Wilf Meek live up here somewhere?" I asked.

"Ay that's right.....'im lives on up this road...nearly at the top of the hill", replied Tony.

As they passed through Ruardean, Harold and Tony discussed Taffy Gardiner's idea for catching salmon. Taffy reckoned he knew the pools down on the Wye where the big fish rested at low tide. All that was needed, according to him, was a 12 foot long net with a man on either end and another in the middle. The plan was to wade through these shallow pools and corner the salmon using the net.

"I suppose you could stitch some muslin cloths together", ventured Harold, "it would make a sort of net".

"That's not a bad idea", replied Tony enthusiastically, "I'll get our Dave working on it".

He handed a cigarette to Harold on the strength of his idea and then lit one for himself as they descended Catshill. The turning to the left at the bottom of the hill was very severe indeed; Harold was wise to turn right and then park on the grass verge overlooking the river. The 'Wyelands' was an old stone-built house located on the side of the road about 50 yards back. We strolled down slowly and entered the house. There were already a dozen or more people mooching about, lifting the lids on boxes and trying out different tools.

It seemed that the better tools were kept indoors whereas some of the cheaper stuff was piled up in chests out in a securely fenced garden area. We went out there and were met by the biggest Alsatian dog I had ever seen.

"Alright boy....alright...", said Harold reassuringly.

The dog looked us over before padding back into the house.

"Wouldn't want to meet that beggar on a dark night", commented Tony with feeling.

Much of the stuff on sale seemed to be Army and Navy surplus; the boxes in which the small tools were stored were in fact old ammunition boxes. Some were half full of rainwater and the contents well rusted. However, we were able to get hammers, chisels and a load of spanners for just a few shillings. It was certainly cheap enough that was for sure. We didn't mention the place to Dave as we feared he would try and help himself to the tools one night, and there was the dog to worry about.

By late Summer the hay-barns were all full to the rafters. It had been an exceptionally successful year with not a single drop of rain falling on the grass as it dried. Even Violet, who was by then in her twilight years, would enjoy tucking into some of the first class hay during the forthcoming Winter.

Mr Butcher had retired from East Dean at the end of the Summer term. He had been the Deputy Headmaster and had ruled Room six with an iron hand. Maths had been his subject but he only taught the more senior pupils. My only brush with him had been as he force fitted my school cap down onto my head when I first started at the Grammar School. I never did have to confront his reddened face, which at times looked like a beetroot with a covering of snow-white hair. Although he looked fearsome, he had done me no harm at all and so I wished him well and just hoped that his replacement would be a little bit more warm and cuddly.

It was by then almost a month since I had taken a few days off to help with the haymaking. My form teacher had queried my phantom illness at the time, much like others had with Tony and Dave in years gone by.

That evening, Father, Tony and I were trying our best to enjoy the culinary creation laid out before us. It wasn't easy; only Mother knew what it was, the rest of us couldn't really hazard a guess! We picked and poked at what we thought were once potatoes and conversation drifted back to taking time off school.

"What was 'Hunt-'em-up's' real name?" enquired Tony.

"That was Mr Turner", replied Mother.

'Hunt-'em-up' was the nickname given to the unfortunate gentleman whose job was to follow up unacceptable school absence trends. He had done that for many years and covered most of the local primary and secondary schools. His very name struck terror in the minds of all young kids. This may have been due to his appearance; he was a middle-aged man with rather unsmiling wrinkled features like a bulldog, and whose greying brown hair was held down with a generous application of Brylcream. Mothers would tell little tots that if they didn't go to school then 'Hunt-'em-up' would come and get them. It was a truly terrifying prospect for any youngster.

"Who was that girl at Littledean school who was always off with earache?" asked Father, "the one that bloke Turner was always going to see".

"Oh that was Betty Meek", said Tony, "her mother thought onions would cure anything and everything".

Mother went on to explain that Betty's own mother swore by onions and, whenever her daughter got earache, which unfortunately was quite often, she then reached for an onion, the biggest one she could find. She would cut it in half and warm it in front of the fire. Then she would make Betty hold it against the painful ear while she tied a scarf around the child's head. That would hold the onion tight up against up against her ear when she was in bed. God knows if it really did any good, but the whole classroom used to reek of onions when she came back to school!

I had arranged to meet David Holder the following morning on the 10 o' clock bus to Gloucester. We were planning to visit Mr Criddle's antique shop at the bottom of Westgate street. It was not the spindle-backed Windsor chairs that interested us, oh no, it was the swords and bayonets that leaned against the wall by the door. Mr Criddle had a wonderful array of blades; they came in all sizes and shapes from sabres to claymores.

The Red and White double-decked bus strained around the reverse camber on the downhill corner by the Guest House, then straightened up and braked hard as it pulled up outside the George Hotel. My eyes scanned the upstairs section, looking for confirmation that David was aboard before I jumped on myself. Then I spotted his freckled, grinning face in the back seat; the expedition was on.

"How much money have you got?" he asked.

"Two pounds ten".

"What have you got?"

"Just over one pound ten after I've paid the fare".

The bus rumbled on through the village and down towards Elton. It stopped by the Greyhound where Gaynor Holford and her sister Victoria got on. They must have spotted us, as they decided to stay on the lower deck.

By then we had done our sums; we reckoned that we would be able to get a bayonet each with the money jingling in our pockets. It was an exciting prospect, although neither of us had given the slightest thought to how we would carry the things home if we were able to afford them. I think we saw ourselves as a couple of swashbuckling 'Errol Flynns', with blades flashing down Westgate Street and the sound of steel on steel as we fought our way up the stairs on the bus!

We seemed to pull up for passengers at every stop on the way. It took three quarters of an hour to get to the bottom end of Gloucester.

"Come on...let's get off here".

I slid across the seat and David followed; we inched our way down the curved stairway and merged with lower deck passengers who were getting off at the same stop. Steel studded heels clattered on the metal deck and down onto the pavement. We nodded to the Holford girls, then looked at each other before heading straight for Mr Criddle's antique shop.

The shop was totally cluttered and had a musty smell about it. The front onto Westgate Street was quite narrow but it went back as far as a cricket pitch. Inside was the owner, Mr Criddle. He walked very slowly with the aid of a stick and hence spent much of his time sat in an old rocking chair at the back of the shop. He was a very elderly man with a large wrinkled flap of skin that went from his chin down to where it disappeared inside the top of his shirt. He was not a friendly man and eyed youngsters like us with grave suspicion.

We walked up and down the narrow, irregular aisles and scanned what was on offer. There was an incredible choice. Huge, rusty Claymores leant against the side of an old wardrobe and there were bayonets ranging from the knife-like design used in the recent Korean war, to way back with long clip-on swords from earlier centuries. It was an awesome sight, each blade with its own buried history and perhaps acts of courage from past conflicts.

David took a real fancy to a particular bayonet; it had a bright silvery blade which was highly engraved and had what he reckoned was a blood channel on it. The price was £2 10s, a bit beyond his pocket. I really liked an old scimitar; it had an ivory handle with a bit that curved around your little finger. It must have been encrusted with some sort of jewels at one time, but by then they were all missing. With a price tag of £3, it was also outside my range.

We shuffled back outside onto the pavement to discuss the situation. Mr Criddle continued to sit in his chair but peered around some furniture in order to keep an eye on us. We reckoned there was no point in trying to barter as we clearly didn't have enough between us for more than one weapon.

"What if we pay for the one and sort of borrow the other", suggested David.

"And sort of come back next week and sort of pay for it then", I added.

We both burst out laughing with a kind of nervous excitement and hoped Mr Criddle 's suspicions had not been aroused.

David borrowed a pound from me and went back in. He said that he wanted to buy the engraved bayonet and asked if it could be wrapped up for safe transportation. That sensible request seemed to allay Mr Criddle's fears and he delved around at the back of the shop to find some brown wrapping paper and string.

Meanwhile, I lurked near the door. I waited until he was well occupied and then eased the scimitar up under my pullover and walked slowly back out of the shop. My heart was pounding as I waited for some sort of shouting behind me. I half expected to hear cries of 'stop thief' and to get wrestled down onto the pavement. But there were no shouts, all was calm and normal on Westgate Street.

Inside the shop, Mr Criddle was cutting the ends of the string he had used to keep the wrapping paper in place. I carried on up the road for a good 100 yards and waited. David caught up with me a few minutes later with his neatly packaged bayonet tucked under his arm.

"Did you get it?" he asked eagerly.

I lifted my pullover to reveal the sword handle, the blade end was by then shoved right down inside my trousers.

"Bloody hell...you can't walk around Gloucester all day with a sword dangling by your willy".

"We'll get a newspaper or something from a bin and wrap it up with that", I replied.

We walked on up towards Kings Cross, trying to look as casual as two lads could when carrying a concealed sword and a bayonet. On our left was St Johns' Lane, it looked nice and quiet and so we took that turning and kept going for a while. Eventually we passed the back of a shop with a bin full of discarded boxes and packing materials. David picked out a large piece of wrapping paper and brought it over to me. I placed it on the pavement and, after looking left and right, dropped the sword on it and quickly rolled it up.

"Is there any string in there?", I asked, quite reasonably I thought.

"Jesus...what did yer last slave die from?", replied David, perhaps a little mindful of the fact that he had no money left by then and I still did.

We got our ill-gotten gains back home without further incident. David had spent the whole return journey trying unsuccessfully to negotiate half of my remaining £1 10s. In the end I gave him the ten bob note just to shut him up.

That trip was the beginning of a collection of military equipment for both of us; I hasten to add that most of it was acquired quite legally, although not from Mr Criddle. The next time we went into his shop, he chased us back out waving his walking stick and cursing us for all he was worth!

Mother told me after breakfast a few days later that I was going on holiday to St Ives in Cornwall.

"Great...when are we going?"

"It's not we...it's you and Ruth", she replied.

I was shocked initially because travelling alone with an elderly blind lady was quite a responsibility. But as I thought about it, my concerns faded quickly. Ruth was a lovely person and it really was no effort to look after her. She had a sister and other relatives living in St Ives and it was her dream to return and talk again with those who were dear to her.

Plans were finalised by the end of the week and cases packed with enough clothes for a fortnight. Well I didn't really have enough clothes to last that long, but Mother assumed that I would get my few bits washed while I was away. Harold drove Mother, Ruth and I to Gloucester railway station. And, after getting the tickets, we made our way out onto the platform. Mother hugged Ruth and kissed her; she then tried to do the same with me. I wasn't having any of it and took Ruth by the arm. We boarded the train and I found an empty compartment. I put the luggage up into the overhead rack and made sure that Ruth was nice and comfortable.

The train pulled slowly out of the station and I went to the window to give a final wave. It was going to be two long weeks before I saw them again and I was not at all sure what sort of place St Ives would turn out to be.

There were not a lot of passengers on the train and we were on our own for most of the journey. After an hour we opened our packed lunches and orange squash drinks. I had to hold Ruth's arm and steer her to the loo a couple of times, always keeping guard outside until she reappeared.

Many hours passed before we finally reached Penzance station. The train squealed to a halt for the umpteenth time that day, although it would be the last time for us, it was where we had to get off.

Ruth had known all the stations on route. I just told her the names as we passed through each one and she would tell me the next one to look out for. We made a great team; I was her eyes and she knew where we were going.

We got off the train and I held her arm. An elderly couple were stood at the end of the platform. They were both about 60 years of age. The man had a kindly face; he was of medium build but stooped slightly as he came towards us. His grey hair was quite thin and his smartly dressed appearance, which included white kid gloves, made him look a bit like a butler from a big country mansion. The lady was slightly built; she had greying wavy hair and was also smartly dressed. The pair of them would not have looked out of place on their way to church.

The man pointed towards us. I told Ruth that an elderly couple were coming towards us; I could feel her trembling as I continued to hold her arm. The lady, who turned out to be Ruth's sister, was clearly overcome with emotion. She threw her arms around Ruth; it was obvious that it had been many, many years since they had last touched and talked.

"So you must be Danny", said the elderly gentleman, "I'm Fred...and this is my wife Doris".

He pointed to the lady who was by then talking agitatedly to Ruth. They were both really nice people and extremely friendly to me. I think they were a bit proud of the fact that I had looked after Ruth on my own; although I was rather glad that my sole responsibility was over for a while.

It took a further half an hour or so to get from Penzance to St Ives. We parked outside what seemed to be a street full of guest houses at the elevated end of town. Fred and Doris owned one and Ruth was going to stay with them. There wasn't a spare room for me, not for the first week anyway, and so they had negotiated with their next door neighbour for me to sleep there.

The first night was a bit strange. I was alone in a room at a house in which I knew absolutely no-one. The lady who ran it was quite pleasant but certainly not gushing. I got the impression that if I stepped out of line she would have come down on me like a ton of bricks.

The following day, Doris took me to meet her daughter and two grandchildren. The youngest was Nicky; she was a five year-old girl who insisted on smothering me with numerous kisses. It was not the sort of thing a 13 year-old boy really wanted; the more I tried to escape the more she kept on doing it. I was grateful when the grandson came down the stairs. His name was Jimmy; he was 13 years-old as well, and we hit it off straight away.

The next two weeks just flew by. Jimmy and I went out each morning and didn't return until tea-time. We explored every cave and rock-pool, and spent hours on Porthmeor and Porthminster beaches trying to learn to swim. We even got some flippers but they didn't help much; I always seemed to end up like a bionic tadpole in a lead suit. A lot of furious arm flapping just didn't seem to stop me from slowly sinking to the bottom. There were many mouthfuls of salty water and spluttering bouts of coughing as a result. We laughed and laughed and laughed, it was a truly wonderful time.

I really thought that we were on the other side of the world until, towards the end of the holiday, I spotted someone I knew. It was one of the Cowmeadow brothers from Cinderford. He was a pupil at East Dean and was a couple of years older than me. We nodded briefly in recognition and then he vanished into the crowd. I didn't see him again until we were back at school.

The wonderful holiday finally came to an end as they always do. I said goodbye to Fred and Doris, and to Jimmy, Nicky and their mother. Ruth and I then boarded the train at Penzance. We waved from the carriage window as the train pulled out. Sadly I was never to see any of them again; it would be all of 30 years before I returned to St Ives, and by then everything seemed to have changed.

Chapter Ten
First half of 1959

The year seemed to start badly. Pit closures were being discussed in every pub and meeting place. Eastern United Colliery had just been closed, resulting in heavy job losses, and there was plenty of talk that Albert and Edward would be next.

There was also sad news at East Dean; George Butcher had just died. What made it particularly painful was that he was just 60 years of age and had only retired the previous July. He had moved from the top of Belle Vue in Cinderford, where he had lived for three decades, to near Welwyn. It seemed that he had gone into hospital for a minor operation a couple of weeks earlier and was making a steady recovery. Then suddenly he had a heart attack and it was all over. He had taught at East Dean for 34 years and had of course made many good friends with both staff and neighbours. The news had come as a real shock to some of the older teachers.

The Spoken Word competition was a couple of weeks later. Pupils from Drake, Raleigh and Hawkins Houses would read poetry or story extracts in front of the whole school. At stake was the Bevan Cup which was presented to the captain of the House with the most points. It must have been a quite terrifying experience for the readers, who incidentally were nearly all girls. Boys, of course, felt that having to put expression into public reading was gravely unacceptable, in fact we made absolutely certain of never being picked by stumbling horribly at any practice sessions.

The competition would go on for what seemed like hours; the whole school was wedged into the Gym and permitted to sit on the floor. It was extremely hard and uncomfortable. We were all continually shuffling from one cheek to the other, often trying to stretch out one leg for a few moments while taking the strain on the other. During all that time, a series of girls were droning on about something or another. I remember one poem was about Macavity, the Mystery Cat. The reason why I still remember it to this day was because of the incredible effort the girl put into her delivery. Her head was going from one side to the other, then her eyes would open wide like dinner plates and close again to slits as her voice dropped to a whisper. Suddenly her voice would boom out again and a stabbing finger pointed at the audience. For a moment I thought she was accusing me of taking the damn cat!

Eventually the last poem was completed. The adjudicating teachers conferred for some time. There was a lot of nodding and talking in hushed tones. The contestants waited eagerly for the result; the rest of us just waited, our backsides by then imprinted with the grain of the wooden floor.

Mrs Hazell stepped forward to congratulate all the participants and remarked on what a close competition it had been.

"The standards are getting higher every year", she said, yet again.

My thoughts went back, just momentarily, to my English lesson that morning with Mr Hodgkiss, or 'Otto' as we called him from afar. 'Otto' was a young, fit looking chap with glasses and out-of-control long, fair hair which he had to push back constantly using his fingers as a comb. He was rather good-natured most of the time; he would encourage debate in the classroom and allow creativity to flow. Occasionally, however, he would lose his self control; this usually occurred when the boys played him up just a little too much. He would then fly off the handle completely and threaten to throttle any offenders. It was prudent on such occasions to back off rapidly and let him calm down.

'Otto' was in quite a good mood that morning. It was just my rotten luck to be picked on for a spelling exercise.

"Stand up Haines....and spell 'necessary'".

I got to my feet rather reluctantly and felt the heat of 30 pairs of eyes boring into me. My blazer had seen better days and I felt self conscious about both my appearance and my spelling; the result was that I felt awkward and got flustered.

"n...e...double c.."

I only got that far before the whole class burst out laughing. Ann Dykins and Julia Burtenshaw were the nearest to me and they thought it was hilarious. I reddened up considerably and felt the sweat break out on my forehead.

"Quiet everyone".

'Otto's' voice brought an instant silence to the room.

"n...e...c...e.."

There was no more laughter and so I knew I was OK that far. The trouble was I wasn't sure if it was then one 's' or two, so I just had to make a guess.

"n...e...c...e...s...a.."

The whole class burst out laughing again. There was a kind of hysterical edge to it, with most of the others thinking how glad it was me on the spit and not them. I felt a burning sensation at the tips of my ears and thought at any moment they would catch fire. 'Otto' shouted for silence once again. I don't think he had heard my second mistake and I was able to press on and get it right on my third attempt.

"Be seated Haines…..right…Meek A...spell 'necessity'".

Antony managed to spell it correctly first time, although I thought it was totally unfair to give him a nearly identical word after I had paved the way for him. I kept quiet though, just to give my ears time to cool down!

My daydreaming came to an abrupt end as Mrs Hazell announced that the winner of the 1959 'Spoken Word' competition was Drake House. Everyone around me started clapping and cheering wildly. I was just grateful to be able to get to my feet and stretch my aching legs a bit. Still, there would be plenty more opportunity to get the circulation going after school, it was a good three mile walk up over Littledean Hill by the Foresters pub and down through the Odd Marks field.

The rest of the week was very wet indeed. It was still raining heavily on Saturday and the big cup match at Minsterworth AFC looked to be in doubt. Harold peered out from the comparative comfort of the tractor shed, pleased that he didn't have to get the home pitch into a playable state, although he still had to run the line.

Soudley Valley Coaches usually provided the transport for league games. They were given a fixture list at the beginning of the season and turned up for the away games with the required number of coaches. That of course depended on how well the Rovers were doing; two coaches if they were chasing promotion or just the one if it was going badly.

For cup games it was a different matter; it was never possible to predict how far a cup run would go, and so a convoy of cars and vans were used to carry both players and supporters to the away games.

At that time, Littledean Rovers had a strong side and a mighty and formidable set of supporters. Many of them were the ladies of the village – the very vociferous ones. When Beattie Rogers and her daughter June decided to remonstrate with an official he certainly knew about it. Those two were ably supported by Dot James, Annie Powell, Annie Giles and others who spearheaded a battalion of biased Rovers supporters. It was not for the faint hearted! Opposing sides and officials must have dreaded the prospect of playing in front of them.

The convoy arrived at Minsterworth in the early afternoon. It was a village with a population quite similar to Littledean, but, being quite close to Gloucester made them seem like foreigners to us. The changing rooms were in the Village Hall on the side of the main road. Players had to make a dash from their cars to the hall, doing their best to avoid the rainwater that was cascading down off the guttering. The supporters sensibly stayed in their vehicles hoping against hope that it would ease off soon.

The Rovers were in their usual black and white striped tops and Minsterworth were in green. Both sets of players looked apprehensive as they picked their way down the steps from the hall. They then jogged across the main road during breaks in the traffic and headed down Church Lane towards the pitch.

"Jesus...are we going to play on that?" asked Maurice Averall, one of the full-backs that afternoon.

"Same for all of us", replied Roy James as he bounced up and down on the spot, presumably to flex a few reluctant muscles.

Roy, Maurice, Tony and Mel Baker were the defensive back four; they looked across a pitch hardly conducive to good football. It was completely waterlogged and muddy, and there was a sizeable pond just behind the one goal-mouth.

The referee was Cecil Trigg from Cinderford. He was a regular on the local circuit and well known for his fairness, although sometimes the opposition from the Gloucester area thought he was twice as fair to the Forest sides! Cecil decided to start the match despite the appalling conditions, probably because it was a cup match and everyone wanted to get it played and out of the way.

We won the toss and decided to play up the slope for the first half. The hope was that if we were still holding them at half-time, then we would have a really good chance of winning the match in the second half.

Cecil blew the whistle and got the game underway. It was a complete lottery, passing was impossible and players splashed around like dolphins.

"Kick the bloody thing 'Aggo'", screamed Beattie Rogers to the hapless Maurice Averall who had slipped at a vital moment and allowed Minsterworth to score.

"You won't win this sat on your ass 'Aggo'", chipped in her daughter June, "get stuck into 'em".

The heavy rain continued and the pitch just got worse. At half-time the score was three-all. The players trudged to some high ground and chewed on rain-soaked slices of orange. They looked a sorry sight with their soaking wet togs and hair plastered down with a mixture of mud and rain.

"We can still win this", said Tony earnestly.

However, neither the players nor the referee had considered the effect of the Severn bore. The huge and unstoppable Spring tide flowed swiftly up the river. It crashed into both banks sending up spray high into the air as it went; it also ran into a ditch running along the side of the pitch. The ditch overflowed within minutes and the one goal-mouth was immediately under four inches of rather muddy water. Fortunately, it was the Minsterworth goal for the second half.

"Cecil 'aint sending us out again is he?" said Mel, shaking his head and watching the droplets fall from his eyebrows and nose.

"Looks like it", replied Tony.

The two teams lined up for the second half; they looked bedraggled but grim. The Minsterworth goalie had to stand near the penalty spot to avoid the water going over the top of his boots. Even Cecil's whistle was affected; it sometimes made a hissing sound like someone whose front teeth had been removed.

The water had reached the halfway line within five more minutes and players were just booting the ball as far as they could and then splashing after it. By that time the supporters were already retreating to their cars and Beattie Rogers summed up the view of most of them.

"They must be bloody mad....and so must we!"

Miraculously there had been no more goals and, by the time the referee decided to abandon the game, the Minsterworth goalie was up to his calves in water. The only person on the field with dry feet was Harold, who never went anywhere without his wellingtons.

The replay was on the Recreation Ground at Littledean on the following weekend. The conditions were perfect but the result wasn't. The Rovers were hammered bringing their cup run to a decisive end. But the stories of playing in the middle of a bore tide would go on for years!

Harold drove the tractor down the lane and stopped at a narrow spot some 30 yards before the Pike House. He switched off the engine, jumped down and went around to the back of the vehicle. In the tractor box was a bale of straw and an old milk-churn filled to the brim with a strong mix of Jeyes Fluid and water.

He lifted the bale out and dropped it in the middle of the lane. After cutting the strings, he pulled them out, wound them into a ball and shoved it into his jacket pocket. The straw was then shaken out of its compressed slices and spread across the entire width of the lane. Harold then wrestled the heavy churn of disinfectant down out of the tractor box and started tipping it onto the straw. He went around methodically, ensuring that the entire area was well soaked. When that was completed to his satisfaction, he restarted the tractor and went back to join Tony, who was busy sorting out suitable containers to be used as disinfectant foot-baths. These were earmarked for all the pedestrian entry points to the farm.

It was a worrying time; Foot and Mouth disease had been reported on Jack Batt's farm in Mitcheldean. We had been so lucky during the previous outbreaks in the area; farms all around us had lost all their livestock while our animals had been spared.

Tony loaded the foot-baths onto the tractor. He then went back for a number of 'Keep Out' signs and a hammer and staples before setting off towards the George Lane. There were quite a few stiles connecting the public footpaths across the farm and every one had to be sign-posted if we were to escape again.

My thoughts drifted back to the previous outbreak just over two years earlier. At that time there had been confirmed cases right across the county, but it had been particularly bad in the Forest.

There was a small field on the edge of the wood down by the signpost at Greenbottom. It was not much more than an acre in size; it had been reclaimed from the wood at some time in the past and a neat hedge had been grown around its perimeter. It was rather curious to have such a tiny field stuck in the middle of nowhere, but it had been there for as long as anyone could remember and we had all got used to it. The animals with suspected Foot and Mouth were taken to that little field.

A large bulldozer turned up one day and started to scoop out a long, shallow trench. It worked away for hours, eventually getting so deep the driver had to create sloped ramps either end to be able to get in and out. By the time he finished you couldn't see the digger; the only thing visible was the smoke from the top of his exhaust-pipe. Bright red earth was piled up in huge mounds at either end and the worm-eating birds in the area swooped in for a very unexpected treat.

The wood surrounding the little field contained mainly mature oak and beech trees. And, after school each day, I crept down through the wood and climbed one of the huge beeches that overlooked where the bulldozer had been working. The tree had a long, low bough with forked branches part way along it. That spot afforded me a comfortable seat and allowed me to peer through the foliage without anyone in the field being able to see me.

More and more sheep arrived each day; they grazed away on what grass there still was after the bulldozer tracks had chewed up and covered much of it. I watched in silence as men built pens along the one side of the huge trench and as the last of the lorries arrived with more sheep.

It was the third day of the activity and I was back on my perch. I watched the men drive as many sheep into the pens as they possibly could; they were crammed in so tightly that not a single one more could have been squeezed in.

Then it started. The slaughterers stepped in with their single action humane killers. They looked a bit like WW2 automatic pistols in shape, but had to be loaded with a .22 calibre blank bullet which caused a retractable steel pin to come out of the 'barrel' when fired. The 'gun' would be held against an animal's head and, when fired, the pin would enter the brain bringing about an instant death.

They waded into the sheep which at that stage were unable to move. The slaughterer would shoot one animal and reload while a helper threw the carcass down into the trench. Those teams worked non-stop in a frenzy of activity. Sadly, some sheep seemed to be still kicking as they went into the pit; I hoped it was just a twitching reaction and that they were well out of it by then.

The work went on for hours; I just could not bring myself to move. It was a truly awful experience, one I recall every time Foot and Mouth hits the Forest area.

That whole event was now history. Luckily for us, the latest outbreak had not been as widespread as the earlier ones and the extent of slaughter was much less than first feared. We escaped again and, within a few months, the foot-baths were all collected in and the warning notices removed from the stiles; it was a great relief to get back to normal once more.

"What do you want wrong with you?" asked Dave.

My brother was holding a notepad against the steering wheel of his Bedford Dormobile van and had a pen poised in the other hand.

"Better make it a stomach upset", I replied.

He addressed the note to my form-teacher, Mr Brown, and explained in the text that my absence from school was due to a sudden and very nasty tummy problem.

"Whose signature do you want on it?"

"Better make it our old chap's....he never writes any excuse notes so that'll be safest way to play it".

Dave made a flourishing attempt at Henry Haines' signature and handed it to me. "Will that do?", he asked.

"Looks good", I replied, "very good in fact".

I jumped down from the van, shouted cheerio and slid the door across. I folded the note carefully, placed it in my satchel and started walking the 300 yards or so to get home.

It had been nearly nine hours earlier that day when Dave and I had arranged to meet on the George Lane near the old Isolation Hospital. I had fancied a day off school and he was more than happy to take me with him, as long as it didn't happen too often. He was by then a service engineer with a firm that produced hydraulic lifts for garages and factories. His area was the Midlands and South Wales and it was work he enjoyed.

I had set off for school as usual that morning wearing my uniform and with my satchel slung over my shoulder. Everything had to look quite normal or else Mother's suspicions would have been aroused. I walked out of sight and waited. Dave had turned up ten minutes later and we headed off in the direction of Birmingham.

Our first stop was at the huge Rover car works at Solihull. There was a lot of security with gate-police and barriers. I don't suppose the fact the service engineer had a schoolboy in tow exactly helped, but eventually we were let in and escorted through various workshops to the lift that required attention. Dave worked hard and replaced the worn cables. It must have taken over an hour before he was able to demonstrate the successful repair and get the paperwork signed

"Where's the washroom mate?", asked Dave.

Up there on the left", replied the Rover workman, "by the fire exit sign".

We found it without any bother; Dave scooped a handful of jelly-like Swarfega soap out of a large metal container and rubbed it well into his blackened hands. I was amazed how well it worked; a good swill in hot water and clean fingers re-emerged from under the grease and grime.

"Let's get the tools and get that chap to show us out", said Dave as he marched back to the lift with me in tow.

"What's that car there?", he enquired, pointing in the general direction of a mud splattered vehicle that looked like nothing I had seen before.

"Oh that's a prototype of the new car....they stress test them on special tracks to try to identify any weaknesses in the design", replied our Rover contact.

"When will it be out?"

"They don't have a date yet".

I got the impression that the Rover chap wished he hadn't talked quite so freely, as he shuffled us out from there with barely another word. In fact it would be many more years before the prototype car hit the public roads, and by then it would be known as the Rover 2000.

We had three more calls to make that day, all of them were relatively minor repair jobs. Dave had planned a fairly light schedule in order to ensure that we would get back to Littledean around 4.30pm, the time I normally got home from school.

It had been a really enjoyable day; not only had I missed double maths, I had also eaten egg and chips in a cafe in Worcester on the way back.

I walked in through the door trying to look as normal as possible. Mother was in the kitchen and Tony and Harold were enjoying a cup of tea before starting the milking.

"Did you have a nice day?", asked Mother brightly.

"Yes I did", I replied honestly, "not bad at all".

Lightly Poached

Chapter Eleven
Second half of 1959

P olice Sergeant Burtenshaw was quite a sharp customer. He had been patrolling the village one sunny afternoon when he noticed two strangers get out of a vehicle parked near St Ethelbert's church. They looked around rather furtively before heading in through the church gates. He watched them from afar with mild professional interest, half expecting them to turn right up towards the graveyard.

The men stopped, looked around again, then entered the church. Sergeant Burtenshaw's interest increased rapidly; it was not easy to visualise them taking brass rubbings. He walked slowly on down to the school, crossed the road and went up to the church door. He paused for a moment and listened, but could hear no sound coming from inside. The door handle made a clunking noise and the heavy wooden door creaked on its hinges as it was pushed open.

The Sergeant stepped inside and could see the two men admiring the altar at the far end of the church. His footsteps echoed around the empty building as he approached the two strangers.

"What a pretty little church", said the one man, nodding to the lawman in between looks at stained glass windows and the altar area.

"What brings you gentlemen to St Ethelbert's ?"

"Just having a look around Sergeant", replied the other stranger.

The two men could hardly have looked more suspicious. They were searched and found to have linen cloths and cash from churches in Blakeney, Lydney and other areas.

St Ethelbert's was indeed a 'pretty little church', but the strangers were in the wrong place at the wrong time with eagle-eyed Sergeant Burtenshaw on the job!

A few weeks passed by and I found myself tasked to help Tony feed the pigs. It was towards the end of the school Summer break and we were in shirt sleeves because of the lovely warm weather. We used cold water for the pigs' food at that time of the year, although during the bleak Winter months we would make sure it was good and hot for them.

I was busy ferrying buckets from the dairy; each was about three-quarters full of water. It was much easier to carry two buckets at a time, that way they acted as a balance and you were less likely to spill the contents. I placed them down outside the little concrete block shed was used for storing the bags of cow-cake and pig-meal.

Tony scooped two brimming bowls of the meal into each bucket where it floated like a four inch coating of brown snow. He used a short stick to slowly stir the meal into the water and, when it was the consistency of a runny paste, he gave it a ten second, high speed whip to remove the last of the persistent lumps. I kept on refilling the empty buckets with more water while he trudged up towards the pigs'-cots with the full ones.

It was never possible to forget the chore of feeding the pigs. When they were hungry they let you know it. The level of grunting and squealing became louder and more demanding as time went on. By the time Tony poured the mixture into the troughs, they were really starting to complain. Some were up at the cot door with their feet dangling over the top, while others were pacing up and down with frothing mouths.

In years gone by we had used stone feeding troughs and that meant trying to get into the cot carrying buckets of food. You were extremely lucky if the pigs didn't knock you over while trying to get at it. However, when Harold built the new row of cots, he designed a trough into each cot wall so that food could be poured in from the outside, giving the hungry pigs immediate access to it from the inside. It made the feeding job a lot easier, quicker and safer.

It must have taken a good dozen buckets of food to eventually silence all the pigs. When we had finished, Tony turned to me and spoke in between puffs on his cigarette.

"Thou's might as well fetch the churns now".

That suggestion was fine by me; it was the most acceptable chore on the farm as far as I was concerned. Blear's Dairy collected the full churns of milk every morning and left the same numbers of empties on the sturdy wooden bench at the end of the lane by the Pike House. Harold and Tony had built it a few years earlier using old railway sleepers, taking care to exactly match the height of the bed of the lorry used for collections. It was a small detail but one much appreciated by the driver. Each full churn weighed around 120 lbs and loading many dozens of them each day from all different levels certainly added to the amount of lifting involved.

The tractor was still not a very good starter even in the Summer. It was normally parked on the slope by the main barn and that was always enough to run it off. I pulled the throttle lever to half open, engaged second gear and, with the clutch depressed, knocked off the foot-brake latch. The old girl burst into life as soon as I took my foot off the clutch. I increased the revs and took an exaggerated loop across the Common and down the hill towards the Pike House.

I pulled up by the milk-bench and had only just stepped down off the tractor when Sergeant Burtenshaw drove by in his car. He was only about ten yards away and looked straight at me.

"Oh sod it", I cursed, "He's bound to come back and nab me".

I hurled the churns into the tractor box and leapt back onto the seat. I turned that mechanical horse on a sixpence using the independant brake and hurtled back up the lane as fast as I could go. The churns clattered and banged against each other but somehow stayed on board. I screeched to a halt just outside the cowshed and ran in to where Harold and Tony were preparing for milking.

"Burtenshaw has just seen me on the tractor", I shouted in panic and, looking straight at Tony, added, "you'd better say it was you".

They both thought my plight was hilarious and were determined to make the most of it.

"Well...as I've got black hair and yours is fair", said Tony in mock seriousness, "he might just notice the difference".

"That won't do you much good", said Harold, smiling broadly as he spoke, "the tractor ain't taxed anyway".

I didn't hear the last bit, I was far to busy running to the barn to hide. I scrambled up over the bales, ignored the choking heat from the hay, and looked out through the slit windows towards the Common. My heart was pounding away as I waited for the police car to pull up.

I stayed in my sweaty hideaway for a good quarter of an hour waiting for and dreading the inevitable. But, to my surprise, no vehicle turned up and in the end it seemed safe to clamber back down over the bales. By the time I rejoined Harold and Tony, I had the appearance of a well baked scarecrow.

"I expect he will have phoned Scotland Yard by now", said Harold, "they will need their best men on a case like this".

"Ay....under age...no license...no tax......you could get three months", said Tony in between whistling noises made by sucking air through his teeth.

It was just too much for Harold, he turned away in an attempt to hide the broad smile on his face; the trouble was his shoulders were already shaking long before his stifled snorts broke into uncontrollable laughter.

Tony was doubled up by then and Harold wiped away the tears that were running down his cheeks.

"Thou doesn't need to worry old butt, he has got more important things to worry about than you".

I could see that they were going to start laughing again and decided to slink off back up to the bungalow.

"What on earth have you been doing?" asked Mother.

"I was fetching the churns and Sergeant ..."

"I mean why do you look like a rag-bag?"

My mind raced ahead. She wasn't asking about the churns incident at all, so Sergeant Burtenshaw couldn't have phoned.

"Oh...I was just up in the barn", I muttered.

"Then get yourself cleaned up before you think about tea".

We never did hear any more from the police; Harold had been quite right; they did have more important things to worry about before nabbing youngsters for doing farm-work – thank goodness!

Dave turned up just after lunch the following day. He parked his Dormobile van by the barn and strolled up to the bungalow. Bob barked loudly as the wrought iron gate clanged shut, but then stopped the moment he saw who it was.

"Alright then boy.....steady on there..", he said as he wrestled the dog back down to the ground and wiped the dribble off his pullover.

He walked in without knocking and found Harold and Tony just rousing from their mid-day siesta. Mother was working out in the kitchen but came back into the sitting room when she heard them talking.

"Would you like a couple of nice trout?", Dave asked.

"I certainly would", she replied, "I just love a bit of fresh trout".

"Then I need to borrow our Tony and our Dan for an hour; I need a bit of help to collect 'em".

Harold's one eyebrow rose about two inches up his forehead. He said nothing, but knowing Dave's track record, he thought all the more.

"No more than an hour mind", said Mother, her brain clearly seduced by the idea of a sizzling trout".

We were out through the door within seconds.

"Where are we off to?" I enquired.

"Down to Flaxley", replied Dave, "and grab your wellingtons... you'll need 'em".

We jumped into the van and tossed the boots into the back. And, as we drove down through Greenbottom, Dave outlined how we were going to get the trout. He had got the information from 'Taffy' Gardiner, so we just hoped the scheme was going to be better than the earlier failures at catching pike and salmon!

As we approached the Gunns Mills road junction, Dave used the column change to ease into second gear and turned then right towards Flaxley.

"They've got a well in that place there", I said, pointing to a rambling old house on the left, "and the water is always ice-cold, even in Summer".

I was soon going to realise how prophetic those words were. In the meantime, Dave had driven around the next bend and pulled into a lay-by on the edge of Welshbury Wood. He turned off the engine and looked around nonchalantly. There was no-one in sight, not even another car.

We put on our wellingtons, crossed the road and climbed over the low fence on the other side. In front of us was a strip of pasture about a 100 yards wide; it ran more or less from the Gunns Mills turning right down to Flaxley Abbey in the distance. On the far side of the pasture was a wood which rose up steeply up the other side of the narrow valley.

We strolled across the pasture and, as there were no animals grazing, the grass was lush and full of wild flowers. There was a quaint old pair of cottages on the edge of the wood; it must have been an eerie place at night as there wasn't another house in sight and it was a long way from the road. The cottages had been built near a shallow but fast flowing stream which hugged the edge of the wood as it meandered down past the Abbey and on in the general direction of Westbury.

The stream was edged with small bushes and trees, the roots of which had been exposed by the fast flowing water and there were lots of hollows underneath them.

"Right then boys", said Dave with the kind of authority that came from being the only one who knew what we were supposed to be doing, "roll up your sleeves as far as you can".

Tony and I looked at each other; it was hard to see much optimism in our expressions. Dave stepped down into the stream and started reaching under the roots with both hands. He worked his way slowly down the one bank and suggested that

• *Our hands were numb and the trout were very small.*

Tony and I did the same down the other.

"Christ....this water 'aint half bleeding cold", complained Tony, and as an afterthought asked, "how are we supposed to catch the damn things anyway?"

"Just feel slowly along under the roots", replied Dave, "if there's a trout in there it'll feel like pushing an apple in a bucket of water, and, if you're gentle enough, you can ease your both hands underneath and grab it".

"A bit like this", he said a few seconds later, triumphantly holding up a wriggling, six inch long trout for us to see.

He tossed it well away from the bank and took out his penknife. He then selected a thin branch on a Hazel bush and cut it off .The side shoots were all trimmed neatly bar the one on the end When he had finished, Dave then retrieved the small trout and threaded in onto the stick before resuming 'tickling'.

The water was unbelievably cold even though it was a boiling hot day. It was impossible to keep your hands and arms under water for more than a couple of minutes at a time. I looked down at my numb, bluish coloured forearms and tried rubbing them with cold, wet hands to get the circulation going. Tony was stood in fast flowing water that came within an inch or two of the top of his boots; he too was suffering from numb limbs, maybe that was why he stumbled slightly and his one wellington filled with water.

"Damn and blast it", he cursed. Fortunately he didn't see the amused look on Dave's face.

One thing was for sure, we wouldn't be leaving for a while; Dave would never give up that easily, and besides, he had enjoyed a bit of success and that kept him going. Soon he caught another and then Tony managed one as well. I cursed their good luck and moaned about my perishing hands until at long last, I managed to catch a tiddler. Suddenly it was all sunshine and smiles, the moaning stopped and it began to be good sport.

Between us we must have caught maybe a dozen trout, although none of them were much bigger than six or seven inches in length. It was not surprising really, the stream was shallow in many places with little waterfalls over rocks and roots, and could not have supported anything much bigger. However, they made a tidy haul when all of them were threaded on the nut-stick.

It must have been nearly two hours before we got back to the bungalow. Dave took half of the fish in for Mother; she was absolutely delighted and didn't even notice how long we had been away.

Tony hurried down to join Harold for the milking while Dave ambled down to the chickens-cot near to the tractor shed. He selected a young bird, grabbed it and carried it to his van with his hand clamped over its beak. He tossed it over into the back where it squawked loudly and looked rather indignant at its rough treatment. Dave drove back to Mitcheldean with his tea on the passenger seat and his Sunday lunch behind him. What a toe-rag he was!

A week later and school had restarted after the Summer break; it was a difficult readjustment to make after being free to do whatever you wanted for so long.

I was a bit out of favour with David Holder because I had accidentally shot him with a pellet gun. In retrospect it had been an extremely stupid and dangerous thing to have done and could easily have caused permanent injury. As it was, a ricochet off the side of a trailer had hit David in the chin, splitting it open and giving him a permanent dimple. He had trudged home from the farm dabbing his wound with a grubby handkerchief, calling me some choice names as he did so. I apologised profusely but to no avail; it was going to literally take time for that wound to heal.

Meanwhile, a new member had joined our little band at East Dean, John 'Pubber' Williams was his name. Everyone called him 'Pubber' because his parents ran the Foresters pub up on Littledean Hill. It was a superb location, enjoying panoramic views of the Severn basin in the distance and Welshbury Wood, Chestnuts Wood and the Roman Camp in the valley just below.

People said that the Foresters had the longest bar in the area. I wasn't sure if that was right, but it could certainly accommodate quite a few pairs of elbows on a Saturday night!

The potential of the pub had not really been developed, it remained much as it had always been, a drinking house for the men. There was a tiny and musty lounge area with a row of old bus seats that had been salvaged and fitted for customers' comfort. It was rarely used, and then only by courting couples looking for a quiet place in the dry. The bar area was indeed huge; it was plain and smoky with a red tiled floor; it was where the men supped their ale.

'Pubber' was not much of an academic, in fact most of us thought he was quite mad. And, despite his being rather good at sports, he fitted in well with our gang and was very popular. He was tall and athletic, with short, brown wavy hair and a carefree attitude to everything and everybody. He had the habit of grouping various odd words off the television and coming out with idiotic expressions like 'hypodermic after the fact'. He had a whole collection of such sayings which, if repeated often enough, could exasperate you beyond belief.

Sometimes we would skip a lesson or two and pop up to the pub where we would sneak into the skittle alley to keep well out of the way. The alley was separate from the main pub and we were able to practise our bowling skills without alerting anyone. We would literally spend hours bowling at four pins arranged like cricket stumps with a bail across the top. The idea was to hit out the middle pin without dislodging the other two pins or the bail balanced on top of them. Over time we became rather good at it.

We were in the school yard one day when 'Pubber' made a suggestion.

"Let's go swimming tomorrow down at Soudley ponds".

"Oh I don't know....I can't swim very well", I replied in a not very enthusiastic way.

"Well I'll teach you.....by the end of the day you'll be able to do a width....that's a promise", he added emphatically.

The next day was Wednesday and class Lower 5A had double maths in the morning and double physics in the afternoon. 'Pubber' had caught me at the right time.

"OK....where shall we meet?"

""Outside the Royal Oak at half past eight", he replied, "and stick a towel in your satchel".

The Royal Oak was on the top of Littledean Hill and was the next pub along from the Foresters; it was a place where we could both legitimately meet on route to school. The plan was to then cut down over the fields to bypass Littledean and come out on the Soudley road near the old Grange.

The following morning was dry and warm as the weatherman had predicted; that at least gave us a chance to enjoy the day off without having to seek shelter too near to civilisation. I reached the agreed meeting place on time but there was no 'Pubber' to be seen. Ten minutes dragged by and I was starting to curse; it looked as if I would be going to school after all.

Finally he came into sight with a bulging satchel slung over his shoulder.

"Where the hell have you been?"

"Oh I overslept", he replied vaguely, then added, "how much money have you got?"

"You useless beggar", I said, shaking my head, "about two bob or so...why?"

"I've got some crisps from behind the bar.....so you can buy the Mars bars".

The fact that he hadn't paid for the crisps didn't seem to matter to him; he felt that he had done his bit and the rest was down to me, even if I had to stump up some hard earned cash.

We removed our school ties and caps and stuffed them in our pockets before hopping over the stile opposite the Royal Oak. A few dozen sheep scattered as we moved speedily down over the fields and out of sight of the road. We took a wide loop around 'Geogger' Allen's house, just in case his wife recognised us, then cut down through Lionel Virgo's fields before coming out by the Grange. A pair of jackdaws took off from the ivy covered ruins and flapped away into the distance.

• *The Old Grange near Littledean.*   Photo courtesy of Roy Mills.

It was another mile or so down to the first of a line of small ponds. It was lucky for us that the Soudley road was very quiet that morning and we only saw a couple of vehicles. As soon as we reached the nearest pond we were able to take the path through the wood and, for the first time, felt quite safe. I glance at my watch and noticed it was just time for Mr Brown to start the double maths lesson; suddenly it seemed to be a wonderful day.

"When is Wilfie Middlecote going to ride that hoss then?" asked 'Pubber'.

Wilf was George Middlecote's oldest boy and was an apprentice jockey with trainer Monty Smythe at Whitsbury in Hampshire. George had told us when he was building our bungalow that he was hoping to get his son into riding. It was a plan that had come to fruition and the whole village was waiting on his first public ride.

"On Friday...how do you know about it then?" I asked, bearing in mind that 'Pubber' didn't live in Littledean.

"Cos they were all talking about it in the bar last night....they reckoned he was riding some time this week".

One thing was for sure; Wilf's brother John, and sisters Mildred and Kathleen, were going to be with their dad listening to the Apprentice race at Kempton Park on the radio later in the week.

We walked slowly and had already eaten a bag of crisps each by the time we reached the main pond. The water looked cool and inviting. Only the occasional dragonfly or bug broke the smooth, glassy surface and sent out small circular ripples. The pond was roughly 40 yards wide by 150 yards long with reeds and pond-weed providing plenty of hiding places for the numerous fish.

The far end was known as the 'floodgate' end, it was where the water was deep enough for diving. However, with my limited swimming ability we decided to stay up at the shallow end. It had the added advantage of being well concealed from any prying eyes down on the road.

We stripped down to our pants and edged into the water. It was teeth-chattering cold even at that time of year. I eased down into it rather tentatively, knowing it would take my breath away. Behind me there was an almighty splash as 'Pubber' did his 'Johnny Weismuller' bit and broke into a powerful free-style stroke that took him quickly over to the other bank.

I just waded out until the water was chest high, then turned and attempted the breast-stroke back to the near bank. The trouble was that I could never seem to get any forward momentum; the faster I paddled the less I seemed to move. After about ten frantic strokes, I always sank slowly to the bottom. Invariably, I took in a mouthful of pond-water and came back to the surface coughing and spluttering.

This went on for half an hour; I was getting no better despite 'Pubber's' coaching and he was getting exasperated. Then he had an idea. He swam over to where two large logs were floating near some reeds. They were roughly eight feet long and about eight inches in diameter with sawn-off ends. They must have been Forestry Commission logs that had been snaffled by other lads for water games.

"Get yourself onto these two".

He was gasping from his exertions as he pushed the logs into the shallows.

"Get one under either arm and kick your legs like this".

He demonstrated a frog-like action that I was able to imitate. To my great surprise and utter delight, I started to move.

"We'll take it nice and easy and go down to the floodgates", he said with an air of supreme confidence.

I edged my way out into the middle of the pond. I was doing a kind of breast-stroke that seemed to work well with the extra buoyancy. 'Pubber' swam alongside as I neared the deep end. The tricky part was getting out of the water and onto the stone-edged bank without losing my footing as I discarded the logs. However, when I eventually stood up on terra firma once more, I felt a strange feeling of exhilaration at being able to say that I had gone from one end of Soudley pond to the other; even if it was with a bit of help!

As we walked back up the path to where our clothes were hidden, I started to feel some pain under my arms. When I looked I found that my armpits and sides were red and raw; the cold water had numbed the feeling when I was doing it, but it was becoming quite painful as I got warm again.

"Look at my arms.....they're raw".

"Ah it's nothing", said 'Pubber' with complete disdain.

Later we went to the village shop and bought two Mars bars; the wrappers were off them before we even got outside. We then messed about in the woods for the rest of the day and, at about 3 o'clock in the afternoon, we started to slowly make our way home.

We arrived at our respective homes at the normal time and no-one was any the wiser. My arms were hurting much more by then, but I was hardly in a position to ask for help or even to let it show.

I scribbled an excuse note for my form teacher, Mr Jones, trying my best to sign 'Alice Haines' with the same flourish as Mother's own hand. It seemed sensible in the circumstances to use my painful arms as the reason for absence, and was rather pleased with my own explanation of having fallen off a fence.

When I got out of bed the following morning I could hardly move my arms. The reddened areas from the day before had become scabby and extremely painful to touch. Luckily, I managed to find some bandage without Mother seeing me and wound it around my upper arms. It helped a lot; at least then my raw arm wasn't rubbing on my raw side.

I handed my note to Mr Brown the following morning. He read it, glanced at my obvious discomfort, then motioned me to sit down. He then called the morning register while I tried frantically to find out what we had done in class the previous day. At first break I saw 'Pubber' again.

"How's your arms?"

"Bloody painful", I replied.

"Doesn't be such a babby".

With that he was off; thank goodness he didn't smother me with too much care and concern!

On Friday there was a loud groan across Littledean. Wilf Middlecote had trailed in well down the field on 'Dicky Bird' in the Apprentice Handicap; he had not been destined to get off to a winning start in his riding career.

Chapter Twelve
First half of 1960

I always felt a strange optimism when the Winter months were behind me. There was no specific reason but I did have a kind of 'feel good' factor when the one end of the school yard was a mass of cherry blossom. For most of the year we were just surrounded by rusty railings, but for a couple of brief weeks in Spring there was the most beautiful mass of pink petals.

Every year, our Art teacher, 'Pussy' Smith, would pick a number of sprigs and take them into the classroom. There we all attempted to do a water-colour painting and somehow capture the freshness and beauty of the blossom. We rarely succeeded; however if 'Pussy' saw a spark of talent or creativity in someone's work, he would spend 15 or 20 minutes of one-on-one discussion with the pupil. During that time the rest of the class descended into anarchy; things were being thrown, boys were running wild and generally going over the top.

'Pussy' was an absolute gentleman; he deserved a more attentive class than he usually managed to get. He was a middle-aged chap with out-of-control dark wavy hair and a generous moustache. He was not from the usual mould of hard-faced disciplinarians; he operated at an artistic level and tried to release the potential of each and every pupil. His drawings were superb; sometimes he created chalk drawings on the blackboard. They might be architectural or still-life, but they were always brilliant. It was heartbreaking to see him take the rubber and, with slow side to side movements, erase a wonderful drawing that the rest of us could only dream of producing.

The advent of Spring also meant Mr Goddard would be after us to achieve 'standards'. These were heights, distances or times that were considered by him to be the standard performance for a given age of pupil. For the under 15 boys that might be say 3' 9" for the high jump or 14.5 seconds for the 100 yards. We were each given a card on which a record was kept of independently verified achievements. Our gang hated doing standards; it was considered quite a letdown to actually be cornered and made to successfully achieve a standard.

On 'athletics afternoons' we all came out with a variety of excuses; they ranged from forgetting your kit through to having a credible excuse note, or even just going missing on route to the new sports field which was located not far from the Foresters pub.

Mr Goddard couldn't be everywhere at once, although he did try his level best to do so. The secret as far as we were concerned was to keep one step ahead of him, anticipate his next move and make sure that we were nowhere to be seen. On the occasions he did catch up with a number of us, he usually made us pull the heavy roller up and down the cricket square. I didn't like that at all, it was far too easy for Mr Goddard to glance over to check for continuous movement of the roller. It made skiving very difficult indeed. As an additional deterrent, he had a nasty habit of making us run a 440 yard lap around the track if we were caught idling. A full lap under the amused gaze of the entire Lower Fifth was both humiliating and exhausting; it was to be avoided at all costs!

We were back on the roller one sunny afternoon; David Holder, 'Benny', Meek A and D, 'Flowery' and myself were straining like cart-horses and cursing our rotten luck.

"Why don't you lot come down and join the Army Cadets?", asked David Holder in between puffs.

"'Cos we would look as bloody soft as you", replied 'Benny' who was clearly not too impressed with the idea.

David had been on about Army Cadets for some time; he had joined several months earlier and had been promoted to the rank of Lance Corporal. It had convinced him that a career in the Army was going to be the thing for him, although he was on his own as far as that idea went. I had seen the Cadets marching along Valley Road a couple of times before with a band of little kids running alongside them singing....

"We've joined the army now,

learned to milk a cow..."

That sort of incident had not made me keen to join up, however, David did not give up easily and continued with his sales pitch.

"We go off .303 shooting regularly...and there's a two week camp every Summer......".

The others weren't showing the slightest interest and so David was by then directing his comments to me.

"What night is it?"

"Tomorrow night at 6 o'clock...come and call for me and I'll take you down".

"You must be bloody mad", said 'Benny'.

The next day passed quickly, although both 'Noski' and I got Saturday morning detention. I got it for copying his homework which unfortunately had a mistake in it. The end result was that both of us ended up handing in identical, flawed work. He then got detention for 'aiding and abetting'. It was rough justice on 'Noski', but he was not the sort of lad to complain about it.

At quarter past six in the evening, I parked my bike against David Holder's garden fence before going in and knocking on the door. He emerged seconds later; I was astonished at his appearance; he looked like a proper soldier. His brasses were gleaming and his neatly pressed uniform fitted him like a glove. On either sleeve was the recently sewn stripe of a Lance Corporal and, bearing in mind how badly his school cap fitted, it was something of a surprise to see an almost moulded beret with the bright silver badge of the Herefordshire Light Infantry on the front of it.

The image of a mature soldier was dented slightly by watching him struggle to mount his bike and get his hefty boots into the toe-clips. Eventually he managed it and we cycled together down through Cinderford towards the TA Centre at the bottom of Station Street.

"These sodding toe-clips have scuffed the shine off my boots", he complained angrily.

I said nothing; I was far too busy visualising what I was going to look like in a uniform. We parked our bikes and I was introduced to Lieutenant Payne, the CO, and Sergeant Major Smith, whose nickname was 'Thunderguts'. The reason for that became agonisingly apparent when he formed the rag-tag band of cadets into ranks outside the Centre.

"Get into line you 'orrible lot", he bellowed at the top of his voice.

The assembled squad was a sight to behold. Some of the lads I knew slightly from East Dean and others I had seen before around Cinderford on odd occasions. There was Gerald Sutton and Derek 'Bird's Nest' Giles in the front row; they were both in the year behind me school. They were good mates and were generally to be seen together; Gerald was a good looking lad, stocky and broad shouldered, with his fair hair swept back in an 'Elvis' style. His mate, 'Bird's Nest', was a likeable tearaway who lived at Abbotswood Lodge in Ruspidge. He was tall and thin, quite mad and wore his unmanageable blond curly hair in a huge mop perched on the top of a closely trimmed 'short back and sides'. His nickname of 'Bird's Nest' was an insult to most birds as their efforts were always a lot tidier than Derek's hair!

Next in them was 'Younger', he too had difficulty with his beret. It didn't seem to want to bend down over his right ear and, as a result, stuck out sideways giving him the appearance of a French onion seller. Stood by him was John Taylor, a lad of few words. His eyes looked wild and staring, and his long, lank hair and drooping moustache made him look like a wanted Mexican bandit. Dave Addis was stood bolt upright on John's left; he was sporting a close trimmed carpet of curly ginger hair and cursed everybody near to him. Corporal Witts and Sergeant Hill were on the end of the line, they like David Holder seemed to fill out their uniforms with a kind of smartness that eluded the rest of the squad.

I felt very self-conscious stood there in a hand-knitted green pullover, jeans and a pair of daps. Having no idea what to do was something of a disadvantage, so I just tried to follow the actions of the cadet stood next to me. His name was 'Pudder' Brain; I hadn't met him before but he was friendly in that strange and hostile environment and I was very grateful for any help I could get. 'Pudder' is not to be confused with 'Pubber', who happened to be stood in the row behind with half a cigarette cupped in his hand. He was sharing with 'Hopper' Stevens; the pair of them were taking crafty, alternate drags. I don't know how 'Pudder' happened to get his nickname, but he was certainly helpful. He was short and well rounded - he was not one of Pharoah's 'lean kine'. His stocky build and powerful forearms, together with his 'short back and sides' haircut, reminded me of Fred Flintstone.

I didn't know the other lads in the squad at that stage, however, you can probably imagine what a motley looking crew we were. And, under controlled conditions, we were in due course to be unleashed with .22 rifles, .303 rifles and Bren guns. What a truly terrifying prospect for the innocent residents of Cinderford!

At school the following day we were absolutely full of it; we talked of the proposed Summer Camp in Cornwall and of a shooting competition planned a few weeks later up on the Cotswolds at a place called Seven Springs. I had been promised my uniform by then and was confident that I would look better in it than 'Bird's Nest' Giles.

I walked home that day with 'Pubber'. We chatted until we reached the Foresters pub where he unlatched the wooden doors into his back yard and, after a quick 'cheerio', disappeared inside. I walked slowly on down through the Odd Marks field, where a few of Mr Hayward's cattle stared at me with vague interest, and then headed down over the Grove towards the Pike House on the George Lane. The distinctive smell of sheep's wool greeted my nostrils long before I heard the whirring of the shearing machine.

There several dozen rather bony looking sheep out in the Big Meadow; their newly close-trimmed fleeces looked rather white against their black faces and legs, and indicated what a busy day Tony and Harold were having.

I hung my satchel on the nearby gatepost and went in to see how they were doing.

"Get thee on up home and get changed a bit smartish…. we could do with a hand on the folding and packing", said Harold as yet another droplet of sweat fell from the tip of his nose.

Tony was rubbing his aching shoulder, it was giving him more discomfort than usual.

"That's your damn motorbikes for you".

Harold looked at me and then nodded in Tony's direction. He was referring to an incident that had occurred the previous year. Our Dave had turned up one evening on his old AJS motorbike. He had kept it for Summer use although of course he had the van for work and most of his social trips.

It had been a warm evening, and his arrival had coincided with that of Johnny Hawkins, one of Tony's good mates. Johnny lived with his brother Ray and his parents at the top end of Silver Street in Littledean; in fact their house was no more than 60 yards from where Harold lived. Johnny was a burly young man with broad shoulders and a chest like a cider barrel. His hair was black and well trimmed, with a stylish wave in the front that was held neatly in place, whatever the weather, with a generous handful of Brylcream.

"Alright to take the bike out to 'Long 'uns' and back?" asked Tony.

Dave nodded and disappeared into the house. Tony kick-started the bike and Johnny jumped eagerly onto the back. There was a spitting of gravel as they pulled off in first gear with the throttle full open. They hurtled across the Common in the general direction of 'Long 'un' Brain's house on the edge of Chestnuts Wood.

A dog started barking furiously as the bike roared by the house and turned down a little footpath into the wood. Soon they came to a narrow ditch and, for some reason known only to him, it became a challenge for Tony to clear it. He turned the bike around and went back far enough to get a good run at it. The bike was at maximum revs and in second gear as they approached the ditch with Johnny holding on grimly to Tony's waist.

I think they had miscalculated the effect of Johnny's 13 stone on the back. The bike

Lightly Poached

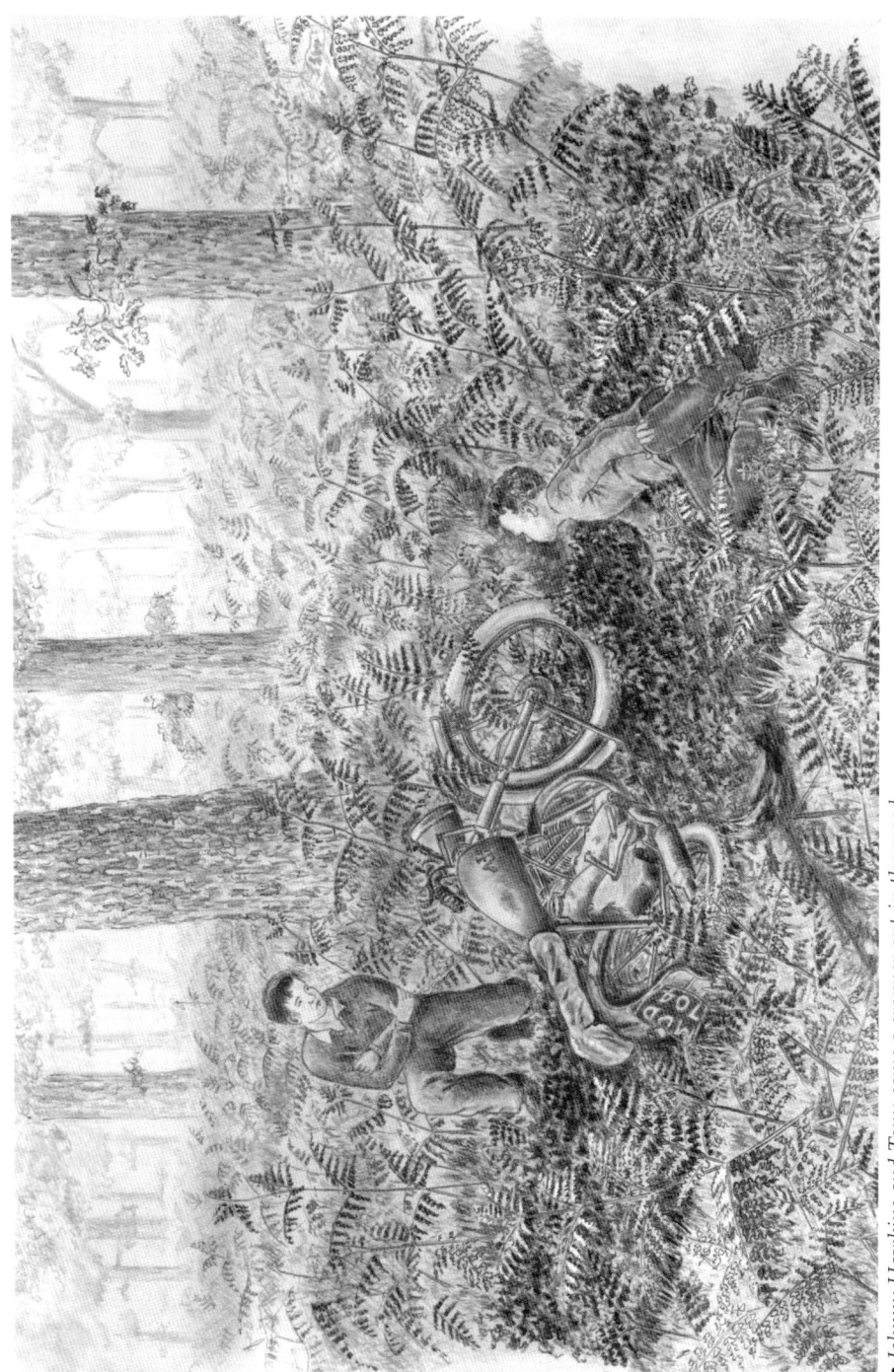

• Johnny Hawkins and Tony came a cropper out in the wood.

never really took off; in fact it just ploughed straight into the far bank and cart-wheeled over. Both Tony and Johnny were thrown high in the air before crashing down into the ferns.

"I think something 'aint quite right", said Tony.

Johnny was badly winded but eventually picked himself up and looked around. Tony's left arm was dangling down by his side and his left shoulder seemed about six inches lower than the other.

"Bloody hell Tone…I reckon thous bust thy arm old mate".

Johnny wrestled the bike up out of the ferns and wiped the clods of earth and greenery off the footrests and handlebars. He was extremely grateful when it started first time and pulled over to where an ashen-faced Tony was standing.

"Let's get thee home".

"There's no car there", replied Tony through gritted teeth, "better take it steady down to Denton's Corner and go up to Harold's place".

Within ten minutes, Tony was sat in the car with Harold and his brother in law, Maurice Buffrey, on their way to Gloucester Hospital. Meanwhile, Johnny restarted the bike again and went back to the farm where Dave was waiting impatiently.

"Where the hell have you been?.....and where is our Tone?"

"The bike is alright", replied Johnny reassuringly, "we came off in the wood and Tony knocked up his arm a bit".

"Well where is he now?"

"Harold and Maurice have taken him into the Hospital".

Mother came out through the door at that moment and looked around. Johnny decided it was high time to vanish down over the fields; he turned on his heels and left Dave to do the explaining.

There were very few people in the Casualty department and a doctor was able to see Tony almost straight away.

"Can you lift your arm Mr Haines?"

Tony grimaced with pain as he struggled to lift his left hand much higher than his waist.

"A bit higher if you can manage it…..that's it….now straight as you can please".

The sweat was by then breaking out on Tony's brow. The doctor took a firm grip on his hand and forearm and, without warning, gave it an almighty wrench. There was a blood-curdling scream as the dislocated shoulder popped back into place.

"Don't do try to do too much with it for a while Mr Haines", said the doctor with a wry smile.

"Yes...that's your motorbikes for you", repeated Harold, "and Dan...look sharp and get changed".

I stopped daydreaming immediately and Tony stopped rubbing his shoulder. He grabbed the handle of the shearing machine and started winding again with renewed vigour, as if to prove that motorbikes had absolutely nothing to do with his aches and pains!

Father had always hated travelling to work into Gloucester on the bus every day. It was also rather expensive even though he bought monthly tickets. Well, he paid for them anyway; I had the job of going to the Red and White bus station in Cinderford to actually collect what looked like a school bus-pass.

"I'm thinking of getting a motorbike", he said one day in mid-Summer.

There was a look of incredulity on our faces as we tried to take in what he had just said. I looked at Tony and he in turn looked at Mother; we could not believe it, Father had never been at the controls of anything other than a ship! The very idea of a 50 year old man suddenly donning leathers and careering down the road on a motorbike was hard to imagine. On top of that, Father did not look very strong; he was nearly six feet tall but looked gaunt with his sunken eyes and thinning white hair.

"What on earth....", began Mother.

Father did not let her finish.

"I reckon that I can halve my transportation costs", he said, "perhaps even more than that".

It wasn't the costs that were causing the mental blockage for the rest of us, it was just trying to visualise Father on the saddle of a motorbike.

"You'll have to take your Test", said Tony, mindful that he and the rest of the motorists on the road all needed protection from a madman.

"Have you thought this right through?"

Mother's forehead was creased and her eyebrows were angled down towards her nose; her expression indicated most clearly the many doubts she had on the whole idea.

"Yes", he replied emphatically, "I shall need Dave and Tony to come with me on Saturday to make sure I don't get done".

Tony's eyebrows slowly came back down over his forehead and resumed their normal position just above his eyes; he wondered what on earth Dave would make of the idea. In fact when Dave heard about it, he didn't believe it, he thought it was a wind-up or that some sort of practical joke was being played on him as retribution for one of his earlier pranks.

When the weekend eventually arrived, Father had already acquired a brown envelope into which he had stuffed a wad of notes. He belonged to the old school who felt that an offer of cash would always secure the best deal. Our Dave turned up at mid-morning and we accompanied Father to the van. Tony and I sat in the back as we headed up towards Littledean. Dorothy Phelps was talking to 'Tuppy' Wynn near the entrance to the Folders Estate; however, they didn't recognise the vehicle as we sped by and turned right to Cinderford.

Our destination was Haines Motorcycles at the bottom of the High Street. The family who ran the shop were no relation to us at all; it was just the nearest place to us that sold motorbikes and they had a good reputation in the area. I had been in there many times before with David Holder or his paper-round partner, John Lugg. We were usually after handlebar tape or transfers for our push-bikes, or else new brake blocks or an inner-tube if maintenance had become essential.

Both Tony and Dave tried out several bikes before they eventually agreed that a 250cc BSA was probably the best one for Father. He had to take their word for it of course as he was unable to ride at that stage. The BSA was a bit heavy for him, but Father was adamant that he wasn't going to have any of that 'Japanese rubbish'.

When the deal had been completed and Father's brown envelope was considerably thinner, Tony rode the bike home with me on the pillion, while Father took the steadier trip back with Dave.

The next few weeks were spent trying to get Father up to speed with the Highway Code and also safe enough to be out on the road. I have to admit that I was surprised by his determination and, although he looked like a 'bag of potatoes' tied onto the saddle, he did stick at it and eventually get to the point where he put in for his Test.

He didn't have long to wait; we were all astonished when it turned out to be only a couple of weeks. And, once he had a time and date for the Test, he swotted the Highway Code book like someone in the final week before taking his GCE's!

On the appointed day, Father took it steady as he made his way down to Monmouth, the town in which most car and motorbike test were taken at the time. He parked up and went inside the Test Centre to check in.

The examiner seemed a rather nice sort of chap and took his time explaining to Father how the Test would be conducted. He emphasised the emergency stop routine, making it clear that he would step from behind a parked car somewhere on the designated route, and at that point, Father had to 'slam on the anchors' while staying in control of the bike.

He started off nervously but Father's confidence rose considerably as his performance continued to be error free. He was three parts through the Test when a man stepped out from behind a parked car. Unfortunately the man was just out shopping; he was definitely not the examiner. He had stepped out only yards from Father who slammed on his brakes and slithered to a halt after just clipping the poor fellow. There was the pungent smell of burning rubber in the air as Father dropped the bike onto the road and bent down to check on the injured man.

"I'm so sorry…you just stepped straight out and I couldn't stop in time….are you alright?"

"Yes I think so", replied the chap as he rose gingerly to his feet, "I just didn't hear the bike at all".

Fortunately the pedestrian was unhurt; he was more embarrassed than anything else for causing such a fuss. Father failed his Test needless to say, although he did stick at it and managed to pass on his next attempt.

Sarah was one of our sows. Her back was creaking under the considerable weight of Billy, the affectionate name for Jack Barrington's Landrace boar. Billy was frothing at the mouth and making curious grunting noises, while Jack and Harold leaned against a nearby gate, taking it easy and enjoying a cigarette. Jack was a bit of a character, his cornflower-blue eyes twinkled as he talked, and that was something he could do for quite some time. Both he and Harold were by then turned 50 and starting to slow down just a bit. Their grey hair and stubbly chins contrasted strongly against their sun-tanned skin.

Jack was wearing an open-necked red plaid shirt that revealed a very hairy chest that was also turning quite grey.

"Who was that bloke down Lydbrook who got had up for watering his milk?".

"I didn't know him", replied Harold, "he must be new to the area".

"Well the beggar couldn't have done much schooling, 'cos he was daft enough to put in more water than milk", chuckled Jack.

Harold took a deep drag on his cigarette and looked out over the fields.

"Well how much do you put in yours then?", he enquired with a broad grin that stretched from one ear to the other.

Jack burst out laughing, "hey mind….I shall take Billy home if you're going to talk like that".

They were still leaning on the gate and talking as I walked by with David Holder and Gerald Sutton. All three of us had 12 bore shotguns cradled in our arms; we were all heading off up into Chestnuts Wood to see if we could bag some pigeons, or if we were really lucky, maybe a pheasant.

"You boys want to watch out for that new gamekeeper mind", shouted Jack.

"Ay alright", I replied, "but he won't bother us".

In fact we had already met the new gamekeeper out in the woods on several occasions. He had moved into Rose Cottage down at Greenbottom and seemed to be a really friendly sort of chap. He was passionately interested in protecting deer, pheasants and newly planted trees, but was quite happy for us youngsters to shoot a few pigeons or squirrels as long as it was out of the breeding season. We just had to make sure that he wasn't around if we were after anything else!

We had been out in the woods for more than two hours and all we had to show for our efforts was one grey squirrel. David Holder had bagged it and was rather proud of his first ever success. Gerald and I had loosed off several barrels without hitting anything and had resorted to target practice at old tin cans in our frustration.

There had been many shooting expeditions like that. We always set off with high hopes but invariably returned empty-handed. Rough shooting was good for exercise but not so good for the table.

"I can't take this squirrel home", moaned David.

"Why not?", enquired Gerald.

"'Cos our mam won't have it in the house".

We sat down on a tree stump on the edge of Chestnuts Wood. In the distance we saw Jack Barrington drive off with the exhausted Billy in the back of his truck. David had placed his squirrel on the grass by his feet.

"I know", he exclaimed, "why don't you skin it?"

I looked up to find that he was looking at me.

"I don't want to skin the damn thing".

"I'll give you two bob if you do", he said as he reached down into his trouser pocket and pulled out a shiny two shilling piece and a handful of fluff.

"Let's have the two bob then".

"No....you can have it after you've done it".

"Hey....if you want it skinned....you hand over the spondulicks first".

David handed over the money rather reluctantly, but it was a 'seller's' market and he knew it.

I managed to skin the creature eventually, although it made me feel sick; it was an awful job and I swore never to undertake anything like it again, not for two bob anyway!

Chapter Thirteen
Second Half of 1960

I could hear the rather slow revs of Father's motorbike from the bedroom where I was sat trying to make a 'pull-through'. It was only a yard of string with a four inch nail tied to the one end and a clean piece of cloth tied to the other, but it worked rather well. After a just couple of squirts of oil had been applied to the cloth, the nail was dangled down the barrel of the 12 bore and pulled through slowly. That process was repeated several times until the inside of the barrels gleamed and had a nice protective smear of oil as well.

I was about to congratulate myself on a job well done when Father started cursing; he had just bumped into the pheasants - again!

"Why are these bloody things still hanging here?"

"They need to hang for a week…to get the best flavour", shouted Mother from another room.

"They'll be full of maggots if they're left up much longer".

Our intrepid motorcyclist was not happy at all and banged his way into the bedroom making the maximum amount of noise as he did so.

It seemed a good time to go and feed my pigeon; it was a 'racer' that had lost its way and decided to stay around the farm buildings where it could get food. The bird seemed healthy enough and had been quite easy to catch. I had put it in a large hen-crate as a temporary home and was just giving it a handful of wheat when Harold walked by.

"You can't keep him in there old butt", he said, "it's far too small….you need a proper loft".

"I know…but we don't have anything suitable".

"That's no problem…we can build one".

"You can't build a pigeons' loft….".

My tone of voice must have conveyed my doubts.

"I damn well can", he replied firmly. "Now do you want me to build you one or not?"

I was really surprised by his wonderful offer and stumbled a bit before managing

Lightly Poached

to say - "yes please".

"Right you are then...I'll see if I can make a start while you are away at that Camp".

Harold was referring to the two week Camp with the Army Cadets; there were nearly 20 of us going from the Cinderford Platoon. We were off to the Penhale Camp near Perranporth in Cornwall, where we would be based with other Cadets from all over the country. I had managed to obtain a money belt and so felt quite secure in what was going to be an unknown environment. David Holder, 'Pubber', 'Pudder' and all the rest of the crew were going and I couldn't wait for the weekend to arrive.

"Squad.....atten...tion", bellowed 'Thunderguts' who then followed on with, "into threes...left...turn"

He looked up and down the ranks.

"You 'orrible creature Private Giles....we'll make a soldier out of you in the end".

There was a lot of sniggering and banter; the Sergeant Major was not amused, or at least he pretended not to be.

"Quiet in the ranks".

'Thunderguts' walked up and down a couple of times and then around the back of the squad.

"Am I hurting you Private Sutton?"

"No Sergeant Major", came the instant reply.

• *Mother left the pheasants hanging a little too long for our liking.*

"Then I ought to be...'cos I'm standing on your hair...get it cut".

"Yes Sergeant Major".

Shoulders were twitching in all the ranks as we tried to stifle our laughter.

"By the left...quick march..."

We marched smartly across the concrete in front of the TA Centre to where two mini-buses were waiting. 'Thunderguts' halted us and let us 'fall out' in order to load our suitcases. When that had been completed and the list of 'campers' checked and confirmed, we set off for Cornwall.

I had always found the Army Cadet uniform to be really uncomfortable. The trousers were thick and heavy and the bottoms were clamped by buckled gaiters; I always had to press them myself and my creases were not exceptional. The tunic was of the same heavy material and the shirts were unbearably itchy to the skin. We were not permitted to loosen ties or anything and the heavy black boots just about maximised the discomfort. The only concession was that we could remove our berets and stuff them under our shoulder straps. By the time we passed Newquay we were soaked with sweat and wishing we hadn't bothered to go. Mercifully it was only another quarter of an hour before we reached our destination - Penhale Camp.

The Camp was situated high above the sea on Penhale Point and had the appearance of a Regular Army Camp. It had a perimeter fence with a Guardhouse; inside were literally dozens of identical, large wooden huts, one for each Platoon.

'Bird's Nest' Giles was the first out of our minibus and he looked awful; the rest of us looked no better and we could only hope that a good night's sleep would transform the lot of us.

The next few days were really intensive; there was endless square-bashing, map reading, target shooting and seeing how long it took you to take a Bren-gun apart and then reassemble it. At one stage we had to take it in turns to shout orders to a squad that were the best part of a 100 yards away. I knew at once that I was going to be no sort of competition to 'Thunderguts'; he absolutely thrived on that sort of thing.

It was wonderful to eventually be given an afternoon off to go down on the beach. Most of the Cinderford mob went down together and splashed around in the not-too-hot breakers.

After a while, we decided to go off and see if we could find a café or pub within walking distance; all of that is except 'Pubber'. He had spotted a couple of rather attractive girls in bikinis and had fallen in love from a distance of 30 or 40 yards. A few of the other boys had tried to chat them up but they were clearly not interested. 'Pubber', however, was not put off that easily; he lit a cigarette and hovered.

We walked back by two hours later and 'Pubber' was still hovering. There was an advert on television at the time by Strand cigarettes; they featured a lone man on a beach and a sympathetic voice echoing the words 'You'll never be alone with a Strand'. 'Pubber' was ribbed mercilessly about it but he didn't care. A few days later we were given some more time off and he was back on the beach again, in love from afar!

There was a major exercise planned during the second week. It involved a long route march by all the Platoons, followed by setting up a bivouac out on some grassy dunes. It was to be a fitful night's sleep for most of us; if Roger Pearce from the Mitcheldean outfit had woken me up once more with his stories and jokes, I'd have cheerfully shot him.

The following morning was spent on a kind of initiative test and, when that was over, we still had to face the long march back to Camp. We certainly didn't have a problem nodding off that night I can assure you.

Maybe it was because we were still tired, but early the next day, both 'Younger' and I failed to salute a senior officer. We were put on 'fatigues' and told to report to the Cookhouse immediately. Neither of us wanted to spend the rest of the day sat by a mountain of potatoes, so it was with great reluctance that we peered around the Cookhouse door.

"We've been told to report to you", I said to a man dressed in white overalls.

"I'm too busy to worry about you two....go and clear the rubbish off the parade ground".

We didn't need a second invitation, even though the man in overalls could have been a painter and decorator for all we knew. We dawdled our way around to the parade ground and found it to be deserted. There were a few scraps of paper which we collected before sitting down on some concrete steps at the far end of the ground.

"There's nobody around", said 'Younger', "why don't we just slope off?"

"Ay...might as well....nobody is going to miss us".

After a casual look around to make sure we weren't under observation from any windows, we made ourselves scarce. We never did hear any more about it; in a Camp that size it was easy to get lost and that was a lot better than peeling spuds all day.

The Cinderford Platoon were on guard duty that night. Each Platoon had to take their turn, and it was our rotten luck to have to cover the hours of darkness. We were dotted around the perimeter of the Camp in pairs; all of us were well rehearsed in shouting, " halt...who goes there?"

Luckily for us it was a dry, still night; it would have been unbearable to be stuck out on those windswept cliffs with the rain lashing into us. As it was, the only sounds I could hear were Gerald Sutton's hob-nail boots stamping on the road as he marched up and down nearby. At two o'clock in the morning I saw something I had never seen before, or since come to that; it was dozens of glow-worms displaying their bright amber lights on the scrub-land outside the Camp fence.

"Hey Gerald...come and see this".

"What is it?" he whispered, thinking we had some sort trouble to handle.

"Look at them glow-worms....they're incredible..."

I pointed to the tiny lights on the ground near the fence.

"Jesus....I thought we had some drunks or jokers to deal with...my bloody heart's pounding ".

We completed our watch without further incident and, after a few hours sleep, we started 'bulling' our boots and getting our kit ready. There was to be a massed inspection of all Platoons on the parade ground, and we had to look immaculate. Immaculate was a very popular word with 'Thunderguts' because on parade you were either immaculate, and that was good news, or you had some fault or another with your appearance, and that was very bad news indeed.

I had always wondered how some of the NCO's managed to get their toe-caps to shine like glass and, because the reputation of the Cinderford Platoon was at stake, they shared the secret with the rest of us.

An electric iron was partially heated up and then used to smooth out the dimples on the toe-cap. Then there was the long, slow process of repeatedly applying black polish, followed each time by rubbing it in little circles with a clean cloth dipped in water or some spit. Every so often the boot was given a good buffing with a dry cloth to see how the shine was coming along. If you had mastered the process sufficiently, then, after a couple of hours, your toe-caps took on the appearance of mirrors.

We all looked damned smart at the final inspection, although to Lieutenant Payne's chagrin, we did not take the award for the top Platoon. I shall always hold 'Bird's Nest' Giles responsible for that failure, because with his beret yanked down over his hair, it didn't matter how shiny his boots were!

There wasn't much conversation in the mini-bus on the way home; we were all tired and weary and ready for our own beds. We were dropped off at the TA Centre in Cinderford and left to make our own way home, each of us lugging a small suitcase. I walked up Station Street with 'Hopper', 'Younger' and 'Pubber'.

"I shall be glad to get these sodding boots off", sighed 'Hopper'.

That seemed curious to the rest of us as 'Hopper' had recently bought a pair of high-heeled cowboy boots that he insisted in wearing everywhere. It was hard to imagine them being much different to Army boots, but we were too tired to argue about it and he then headed home across Church Road anyway.

As the remaining three of us continued our way up through Hilldene we laughed as we recalled some of the exploits of the previous fortnight, particularly 'Pubber's' penchant for Strand cigarettes.

After shouting 'cheerio' to the others, I walked down through the Odd Marks field and had a breather as I sat on the stile at the top of the Grove. However, the view was different to the usual one, there was a newly-built brick and wood building down in our garden.

"Harold has built me a pigeons' loft", I said out loud.

I grabbed hold of my suitcase and ran down the steep path through the Grove , across the George Lane and up to the bungalow. I dropped my case, ran down into the garden and peered in through the wire-mesh windows. They were a kind of box-shaped bay window design that enabled birds to sun themselves. The flat top on them gave a landing area for the incoming birds, who entered the cot by a row of 'U' shaped wires that operated on the same principle as a cat-flap.

Inside was my racing pigeon, all alone in that magnificent loft.

"What do you think of that then?"

It was Harold; he must have seen me coming down over the Grove and kept out of sight to observe my reaction.

"It's absolutely marvellous...how did you manage to do all that in the time?"

"Oh I did a bit here and a bit there....Tony gave me a hand when he could".

"It's bloody brilliant....thank you...thank you so much".

"All you need now is a few more pigeons".

"Yep....I shall go and see if anybody has any spare birds tomorrow".

"If I was thee old butt....I'd change out of that uniform fust".

The next few months were spent visiting every pigeon fancier in the Cinderford and Littledean area. I would ask them if they had any spare birds as I was just starting up and was a little short of cash. Most of them found my request rather amusing; they would take me to the end of their garden and show me their prized racers. They would also ask me a few questions to check if I knew how to feed and care for pigeons properly.

Many of them gave me one of their older birds that was a bit past its prime as far as racing was concerned. Some gave me a breeding pair; from Les Young in Stockwell Green it was a 'black chequer' cock and a beautiful 'red chequer pied' hen, and from the Middlecote brothers up on the Ruffitt Lane, a pair of 'blue bars'.

I was pretty chuffed with my cot of ageing or failed racers, particularly when some of the pairs started to breed. I had been told by some of the old fanciers that the birds must be kept in the cot until the young hatched, or else they would simply return to their previous homes.

It was a nerve-racking moment when I released the breeding pairs, particularly when they started to circle higher and higher. I needn't have worried however, within five minutes they were back tending to their squabs. And, apart from the weekly cleaning out chore, I really did enjoy looking after those birds, even when the Winter months closed in yet again.

It was one day a little later in the year when I discovered Tony shadow boxing in the cowshed. He was apparently demonstrating to Harold how Randolph Turpin used a left jab and fast combination punches to despatch his opposition. It was an image I was able to recall quite a long time after when the pair of them took me into Gloucester to see some professional wrestling and unlicenced boxing on a mixed bill. The thing that made it so special was the top of the bill clash between Randolph Turpin and Johnny Williamson. Randolph was by then of course well on the slide from the heady days when he had defeated Sugar Ray Robinson for the world middleweight championship; but nevertheless, he had been right up there once upon a time. His opponent, Johnny Williamson, was a local boy who had himself harboured championship ambitions through the mid 50's.

Both boxers were past their peak by that time, but it was going to be fascinating to see if Johnny could take out the ageing ex-champion.

After tea on the day of the fight I pressed on with my homework; it was something we had every evening and a double whack of it on the weekend. When I had finished, I went down to the cowsheds where Tony and Harold were still busy with the final chore of the day. The milking machines were making their usual repetitive slurping noise while the cows just stared ahead and took the opportunity to chew the cud. This continued until no more milk could be seen in the small viewing window on the top of each machine. At that stage, Tony or Harold would prise the 'rubber hands' off the teats and move the machine to the next cow.

It took about an hour for them to finish off all the milking, thoroughly wash the machines and let the animals back into the Big Meadow. After that it seemed to take an eternity for both of the men to get changed and finally ready to go.

Harold turned the ignition key in our recently acquired Commer van and then, at long last, we headed off to Gloucester. I was brimming over with anticipation of a memorable night. It was an uncomfortable ride for me however; I was the junior member of the group and that meant I had to sit on a cushion on the floor in the back.

We eventually arrived at the Sports Hall and parked without too much difficulty. I was tingling with excitement as we entered the large room in which the 'gladiators' were to do battle. I had seen live amateur boxing before but, although I had watched the likes of Mick McManus and Steve Logan on the television, it was my first visit to a live wrestling match.

Our seats were quite good ones; we were about six rows from the front and had an excellent view of the ring. We did not have long to wait; some relatively unknown wrestlers were soon in action - grappling, groaning and banging the canvas to show they wouldn't submit. I was still at the age when I believed all the 'agony' they were going through; I blamed Kent Walton for that because the TV commentator made it all seem so genuine.

The main bout of the evening was the boxing match; it had been saved until near the end of the programme.

The master of ceremonies introduced Johnny Williamson to the crowd. They cheered wildly as the local boy entered the ring wearing a brightly coloured silk gown. The people sat by us reckoned he had trained very hard for the fight. Johnny looked a menacing figure with his greased back wavy black hair and scowling expression. My thoughts flashed back a few years to when our Dave and Johnny had settled their differences amid flailing punches on the dance-floor at the Miners Welfare Hall in Cinderford.

I came back to the present the instant I heard Randolph Turpin's name. The MC introduced him as the former champion of the world as he entered the ring. He still looked fit and lean but his eyes had the look of someone who had seen it all before. He had none of the trappings of his heyday; he seemed a sad, unsmiling figure with his simple white - towel waistcoat; he was by then very much a fallen champion.

Turpin never even looked at Williamson when the referee called them together for the pre-fight talk. They returned to their corners to await the bell. It rang loudly a few seconds later. The boxers took up their guard and circled each other in the middle of the ring. Johnny looked a bit over the middleweight limit and appeared ponderous as he jabbed and looked for an opening.

Turpin was not an easy target and his opponent was forced to clinch quite often. It was noticeable during those clinches how often Johnny took the opportunity to rough up the former world champion; it was also clear that Turpin didn't like the continual 'rough stuff' at all.

Well the 'rough stuff' continued all the way through the opening round until the bell sounded for the one minute break. The seconds wiped away the sweat and jabbered to their respective fighters until the bell sounded again.

It became immediately apparent that there was going to be no more 'rough stuff'. Turpin looked a more determined boxer all together; he looked like someone who going to finish the fight then and there. He manoeuvred Johnny into a corner and then delivered a blinding series of left and right hooks that ripped him apart. Turpin appeared to me to be hitting slightly upwards as if to keep his opponent on his feet while a hard lesson was being taught. Eventually the former champion stopped punching and stepped back. Johnny fell in a kind of slow motion onto the canvas where he remained absolutely still.

We talked about it all the way home. I had never seen anyone taken apart like that before. The gulf between a great ex-world champion on the slide and an extremely hard local fighter, was very wide indeed.

Lightly Poached

Chapter Fourteen
Early 1961

We were all stood outside one of the pig's cots, leaning over the wall and looking at the recently castrated youngsters inside. Father was wearing his usual pair of faded brown corduroy trousers, the crotch of which seemed to dangle a good six inches lower than it should, and the knees stuck out even when he was stood upright. The effect was to make him look even more thin than he actually was. He had helped out with 'cutting' the pigs a bit earlier, it was a job he detested because it made him ill. However, he had recovered somewhat and was still there one Saturday morning in late February, telling Harold, Tony and me yet again what a great idea it had been to get a motorbike.

I don't mind telling you that I was just as surprised as the others that he had actually stuck at it more or less right through the Winter.

"Yes…it was the best decision I've ever made", he said as he took a modest pinch of tobacco out of his tin. He fashioned a decent looking roll-up, dabbed his tongue along the edge and sealed it down. It flared up as he lit it and enjoyed a couple of deep puffs before flicking the used match into the mud.

"I heard that one of Amos Pearce's boys is selling his motorbike", said Harold just to make conversation.

"Is it that the BSA Bantam?" I asked.

"Ay…that little 'un".

""That 'un wouldn't half suit me a treat".

I half spoke to myself as there was no chance of me getting it when I was still barely 15 years of age.

"How much do they want for it?", enquired Father.

"About £30 I think….but I'm not absolutely sure", replied Harold.

"Well…dost thee want 'im?", asked Father who was by then looking straight at me. My mouth gaped open but no sound came out; I was just speechless.

"I think that means yes", said Tony.

"I'll just get my wallet and we'll go and have a look".

Harold, Tony and I exchanged glances and nods; Father's behaviour was unusual to say the least; his glowing love affair with his motorbike seemed to have mellowed him no end.

"I should think our old chap is in a bloody good mood today", said Tony.

"Ay...you'd better snap up thic bike old butt.... before he changes his mind", added Harold.

Harold drove the van with Father sat in the passenger seat; Tony and I were wedged in the back, trying desperately to find something to hang onto as we took some of the bends at speed. I had a silly grin on my face and I just couldn't wipe it off.

Mr Pearce had a small farm up at Pleasant Stile, just outside Littledean village. We drove up past Dean Hall and then turned left down a narrow track. The van came to a slithering halt outside a pair of rickety wooden gates. A dog started barking loudly and made Mr Pearce to come out of the farmhouse to see what was happening.

"Shut up boy", he shouted and, on recognising Harold, came on out through the gate.

"Morning Harold....what brings you up here?"

"Morning Amos....I hear you might want to sell a motorbike a bit cheap".

Mr Pearce chuckled to himself and sent Robert, one of his sons, to fetch the bike from a nearby shed. He wheeled it out and balanced it carefully on the leg-rest. It was a sage green colour and looked like everything I'd ever dreamed of. I looked at the speedometer and noted that it went up to 55 mph; I visualised myself hurtling up along Apple Meadow and rounding up the cattle on my shiny BSA Bantam!

I had been instructed not to show too much interest in the bike and stood clear as Tony kick started it and pulled off up the lane. The familiar 'pop-pop' of the two-stroke engine became gradually quieter as he disappeared out of sight. The conversation was minimal until the engine sound became louder once more as Tony returned and pulled up right by us.

"What do you think?" asked Father.

"Goes alright", replied Tony, "not a lot of power mind".

I remained silent as the protracted negotiations took place; it had seemed to me quite early on they were eventually going to split the difference between the £30 asking price and the initial offer of £20. However, these things had to be played out in full, with neither side willing to concede more than £1 at a time. Father eventually shook hands with Mr Pearce on an agreed price of £25; he then handed over the log book and Tony rode the bike home.

The next few weeks were incredible; every spare moment was spent with 'Pudder' or David Holder taking it in turns to bowl along the fields at full revs. Every so often we had to walk up to the village and get our tin refilled with two-stroke mixture. Mr Featherstone had started up a garage opposite to Court Farm and he supplied the ready mixed fuel for the Bantam. He reminded me a bit of Jack Barrington in that he also fell into the category of a 'likeable rogue'.

Mr Featherstone enjoyed chatting away with us and took quite an interest in what we were doing with the fuel. He gave me a real surprise one day.

"You can take that old bike if you want".

David Holder was with me and together we peered inside the garage workshop where an old, dusty AJS motorcycle was leaned up against the wall. It looked a bit like something that might have been used in WW1 with its huge coiled spring front suspension and rigid frame at the rear.

"Will it still go?"

I tried to ask the question so as not to give offence but at the same time find out if the bike was just scrap.

"Course it does", replied Mr Featherstone with quite a hearty laugh, "you can ride it home now if you want".

I thanked him very much for his generosity and minutes later we were bowling along the George Lane. We didn't bother too much with the niceties of a license and tax and so on, and concentrated on getting off the road as quickly as possible. David was on the back holding onto a gallon tin of two-stroke fuel for dear life as we nipped in through the Apple Meadow gate to safety.

The AJS was a powerful bike with a deep throaty roar and a defective silencer; it make one hell of a racket as we picked our way around the cow-pats and made our way home. 'Pudder' joined us a little later; we then had two bikes between the three of us and that was a lot better altogether.

The following weeks just flew by; it was every boy's dream to be tinkering with motorbikes and racing across the fields; we did enjoy those times.

I was in the school yard one morning talking to Gerald Sutton and 'Bird's Nest' Giles about our exploits on the motorbikes. Naturally, I exaggerated the high speeds a little and perhaps even the width of the chasms I had leapt across, but that was only to be expected as we all tended to 'add a little' to any story. I was in the middle of explaining how David Holder always seemed to get a nosebleed when he came off, when Ken 'Flick' Jones came up to us.

'Flick' had got his name because of the constant care he took to create and maintain the magnificent quiff in the front of his dark brown locks. I reckoned that if he had been the hooker in rugby, he would have come out of the scrum with that quiff still looking perfect! He was a likeable lad, quite tall and slim and a bit shy.

"Here's your pyjamas back...our mam has washed and ironed 'em".

He handed me a crumpled parcel tied up with some old string.

"Bloody hell 'Flick'....what am I supposed to do with these?"

"Stick 'em in your desk out of the way...nobody will take 'em ", he replied, and added as an afterthought, "they're showing the holiday slides in the Biology lab at dinnertime today".

With that he was gone and I was left with a pair of 'Cheshire cats' grinning at me. I felt the need to explain what the pyjama story was all about.

"It was like this....", I said and went on to do my best to cram in the story before the bell sounded and stop Gerald from spreading unnecessary rumours.

Some time earlier there had been a school trip to Interlaken in Switzerland. It had been a cracking trip and we had been given a lot freedom, especially as we were all in a foreign country for the first time. I had failed miserably in Calais when I tried to converse in French.

"Quelle heure est-il?" I had asked with my very best accent.

The chap just shook his head and smiled; it should have forewarned me of my chances of achieving a good 'O' level pass in French. The remainder of the trip was by train, it had been quite good fun until I was stubbed by a cigarette. 'Taffy' Davis had been swinging his hands about while telling a joke and had pushed his glowing cigarette tip onto my chin. It had been a complete accident, albeit an unfortunate one. I say that because in the excitement of it all, together with the newly found freedom, kissing girls had suddenly appeared on the agenda. It proved something of a setback to have a huge scab in the middle of my chin!

We were staying at the Hotel Beatrice in Interlaken. It was a family run hotel on the edge of the small town. The place was bathed in Spring sunshine and was surrounded by beautiful snow-capped mountains. There was the usual chaos at the check-in when a large group of schoolchildren and teachers all arrived at the same time. We just settled down and awaited further instructions.

"Haines, Jones, Lugg......you will be staying in the Annex", said one of the teachers. John Lugg looked at 'Flick' and he looked at me.

"What the hell is an Annex?", whispered John.

"I dunno", replied 'Flick' who was far more interested in his reflection in the window.

The Annex was in fact several hundred yards away. In it were just a few rooms where the 'overspill' from the main hotel were put at peak times. It had mixed benefits; on the one hand there were no teachers to bother us, and on the other we had to walk back to the main hotel for all meals and to be with the rest of the group.

'Flick' was still unpacking although John and I had already finished some time earlier. That may have been due to the fact that our hair needed less attention than his.

"Oh bloody hell....our mam hasn't put me any pyjamas".

'Flick' looked aghast, the Annex was run by two elderly ladies and he didn't want to give them a show!

"Can either of you lend me a pair?", he pleaded with the look of a starving spaniel.

"I only got these", replied John, who was holding up an ageing striped pair of bottoms.

Luckily for 'Flick' I did have a spare pair; I also thought it was better to lend them to him than have to see his bare backside for the next fortnight.

The whole holiday was a fantastic experience of sun, snow and ice, all at the same time. The days just flew by and in no time we found ourselves yet again stood on the platform at Paddington Station. Dennis Sayce, a short stocky lad who had entertained us every day with his 'Satchmo' impressions, threw his case down a little carelessly. There followed a sound of breaking glass and Dennis' round, smiling face took on the expression of someone who had just made a terrible mistake.

Like most of the boys, he was taking a bottle of Chianti home as a present. It had been very cheap but looked rather nice in the raffia covered bottles. However, unlike the rest of us, Dennis had packed his bottle in his case. Moments later, the red wine gradually seeped out and formed a large puddle on the platform. You can just imagine the state of his clothes and the reception he received when he got home!

That had all been some weeks earlier and I had totally forgotten about the loaned pyjamas until 'Flick' had pressed them into my hand. Just then the bell sounded; I shouted 'cheerio' to Gerald and 'Bird's Nest' and I was on my way to another English lesson with Mr Hotchkiss.

The following weekend was partly spent revising for the forthcoming GCE 'O' level exams, and the rest of the time spent motorbiking with 'Pudder' Brain. He had arrived down on the farm early on Saturday afternoon and we had enjoyed the next two hours doing some noisy grass-track racing in the Big Meadow.

From time to time we did venture into the woods, although illegally, to do a bit of 'scrambling' along the narrow, fern-edged paths and over the various humps and hollows in Chestnuts Wood. It was after doing that for a while that I had an idea.

"Let's go down to Flaxley for a little run".

"I can't take this old AJS on the road ..now can I?" he replied.

"We'll hide it in the ferns for now....and you can jump on the back of me".

Within a minute we were edging our way out onto the road near Tibbs Cross Farm. There was nothing about and I opened up the throttle as we went past the phone-box at Greenbottom and on towards the Gunns Mills finger-post. We still had no goggles and the tears were streaming down our cheeks by the time we turned right for Flaxley.

It was the very first time we had been out on the open road and it was an exhilarating feeling. We decided to go on down to the crossroads at Flaxley before turning back for home. I guess we were about a quarter of a mile from the crossroads when a Morris shooting-brake car came by us, travelling in the opposite direction. Sat at the wheel was Sergeant Willetts, the new policeman based at Littledean.

"Oh Christ....we've had it now", yelled 'Pudder', "he saw us for sure....let's try and hide the bike".

I took the left fork at the crossroads, went on for another 100 yards and then pulled off the road into a small parking area near the edge of a copse. We tried desperately to push the bike out of sight but the bank around us was just too steep. Sergeant Willets must have broken the world record for doing a three-point turn, because he pulled up in his shooting-brake before we could make good our escape.

"Oh beggar it all...he's got us", whispered 'Pudder'.

"We'll say we were taking the bike to the blacksmith's to get the kick-start welded".

I was thinking as fast as I could, the kick-start did slip sometimes and so, to make the story credible, I reached down and pulled off the plug-cap. I reasoned, quite wrongly as it turned out, that if he couldn't start the bike then our story might just get us off.

The sergeant didn't believe a word we said and made us push the bike up and down the road as he tried to bump start it over and over again. Unfortunately for him he couldn't, however, as the engine was still red-hot, it just made him even more determined to prove that we were lying. After another half an hour he finally gave up and made us leave the Bantam at Mr Watts' blacksmith shop before taking us back to the farm in his car. It was an awful feeling being caught 'red-handed' and neither 'Pudder' or I said anything on the way home. I got a right roasting off Mother needless to say, and 'Pudder' got the same when he eventually got home. And, when Mother eventually stopped going on about it, I had to go out into the wood to recover the old AJS that was hidden in the ferns!

The time waiting for the case to come to court was spent either revising or doing additional farm chores. I cleaned out the pigs' cots and the cowsheds; I scrubbed out the dairy and even cleaned out the chicken coops. And, when I'd finished that never-ending 'contract' with the dung-heap, I still had to clean out my own pigeons' loft. It was almost a relief when the day of the case finally arrived.

Miss Joan Kerr was in charge at Littledean Juvenile Court that morning. 'Pudder' and I both turned up wearing freshly laundered, white open-necked shirts, grey trousers and neatly brushed hair.

"Make sure you say you didn't realise the gravity of the offence and that you're sorry for the trouble caused", whispered Mother just before we went in.

The proceedings seemed to take ages; Inspector Beasant presented the case and basically emphasised that we were both too young to be on the road even if we were just pushing and freewheeling.

"You boys had better stick to the fields in future", said Miss Kerr when all the evidence had been given, and then added, "a £1 fine each on the riding offence and a conditional discharge on the insurance offence".

We all scuttled back home as quickly as we could, grateful to get off so lightly. 'Pudder's' father wasn't very amused; he had to take a day off work and gave his son a good clip around the ear for all the trouble he had caused.

When the time came to take the exams, I was nowhere near as prepared as I should have been. All of our gang reckoned they had done no revision at all, however you knew it was all bluff and that they had worked really hard.

Each exam was two or three hours in length. We were all seated at small individual tables in the Gym and they were well spaced out to prevent any possibility of copying.

It was a truly desperate moment when the question papers were being handed out – face down. Then came that final look at the clock before the instruction was given: "You may begin".

The first 30 second glance at the questions gave you an immediate feel for your chances. It was really important to then plan out how long you were going to allocate to the mandatory questions, and also which of the optional ones you were going to tackle.

I felt absolutely drained after a fortnight of that intense pressure and was greatly relieved when the last paper was completed. I was in the position of feeling that I hadn't done exceptionally well in any of the exams, but neither had I done too badly. If I was optimistic about it, I could think I'd passed them all, and if I was pessimistic, I could think I'd failed the whole lot. I was just going to have to wait until August to get the official results and, in the meantime, I'd have to start writing off for job interviews.

Our Dave turned up the following Saturday morning with a couple of rabbits for Mother; he was also looking for some company to join him on a shooting expedition. He strolled into the cowshed with his new gun-dog - 'Tinker'. She was a beautiful liver and white springer spaniel whose nose rarely came up off the ground. His old dog, Rover, had been knocked down by a car; it was an accident that had upset Dave immensely, they had been through so many scrapes together over the years.

"Trust thee to turn up when all the work has been done", muttered Harold.

"Best time I reckon", replied Dave as he grabbed a bucket, turned it over and plonked himself down on it. He looked over at the rest of us who were already sat along in a line on the edge of the manger, much like a row of swallows about to migrate.

I could hear Mother's voice in the distance and guessed that she would be joining us shortly. I looked around the faces of the people I knew so well. Nearest to me was Dave who was busy lighting his pipe. Without doubt he was the most incorrigible rogue this side of the Severn. He was by then in his late 20's and, although his marriage to Pat had calmed some of his extreme behaviour, like fighting, he was never going to be a Sunday-school teacher. If two and a half years of torture and hard labour in a Chinese POW camp had not beaten the spirit out of him, then it was for sure nothing else would. Tinker stayed close to Dave's feet and Bob watched her uneasily.

Bob was getting old; there were a lot of grey whiskers on his chin by then and he didn't have the boundless energy that had for years allowed him to race everywhere rather than walk. Harold had talked about getting a new puppy, but had delayed the decision because he knew that the old dog would just 'switch off' when a young one came into the house.

Harold stroked Bob's ears and the old dog looked up at him with the hero worship that somehow all border collies give to their masters. Harold was almost 51 and his hair was a good deal whiter than when we had started the farming venture a decade earlier. His face was lined but he still looked fit and healthy. He tapped the ash off the end of his Players Navy Cut cigarette and smiled lovingly at the dog.

Tony was sat next to Harold; he had become his right-hand man on all issues relating to the farm. He was in his early 20's and was very fit indeed. He still turned out for Littledean Rovers every Saturday afternoon. After the match, he then came back to help with the milking before going out for a few beers in the evening. Farm life suited him and he was very happy with his lot.

"Did you know our Dan has got a Police record now?" he asked.

"Ay I had heard", replied Dave, "Joan Kerr threw the book at him by all accounts".

"If 'er did it was because of all the bloody times you've been up in front of her", I snapped, "it's a wonder 'er don't send you a Christmas card every year".

Dave threw back his head in laughter and revealed his 'tombstone-like' front teeth

"Silly young beggar", muttered Father.

His humour had not improved greatly during the previous few weeks; it had not helped that he was being blamed by Mother for being stupid enough to buy me a motorbike in the first place. He was the same age as Harold but looked a fair bit older. His close-cropped hair was white and his eyes seemed sunken down behind his prominent cheekbones. On top of that, he still insisted in wearing those old corduroy trousers that made his legs look like match-sticks. He was just about to say something else when Mother entered the cowshed with a huge can of tea and a handful of mugs.

"If you're going to be doing a lot of talking...you'd better get some of this down you".

"Just the job Alice....I was just saying how much I fancied a cup of tea", said Father somewhat unconvincingly.

Mother looked at him from under her eyelids. I noticed that there were just a few grey strands starting to appear in her jet-black hair, although she still looked trim and attractive. She had been the driving force behind starting the farming venture as well as continuing to make a business success of it. Nevertheless, the relentless hard work and tough decisions were starting to make her look tired on occasions.

Lightly Poached

"Here's a couple of rabbits for you", said Dave as he handed over some of the spoils from a previous poaching trip.

"Oh thanks", said Mother who was visibly pleased.

"Right then....I'll go and make a cup for Ruth now", she said as she bustled out though the door carrying the rabbits. "And you lot can get on with some work when you've finished your tea".

I took another slow look around the cowshed and the faces of the people sat around inside it.

"Yes", I thought, "they 'aint so bad at all".

I still had to sweat over the exam results for some weeks to come, and then there was the problem of getting a job. What were my mates going to do? How many of them would I see again once I left school? It was a lot to have to worry about.

"Who is coming shooting then?", asked Dave.

Some things were never going to change!

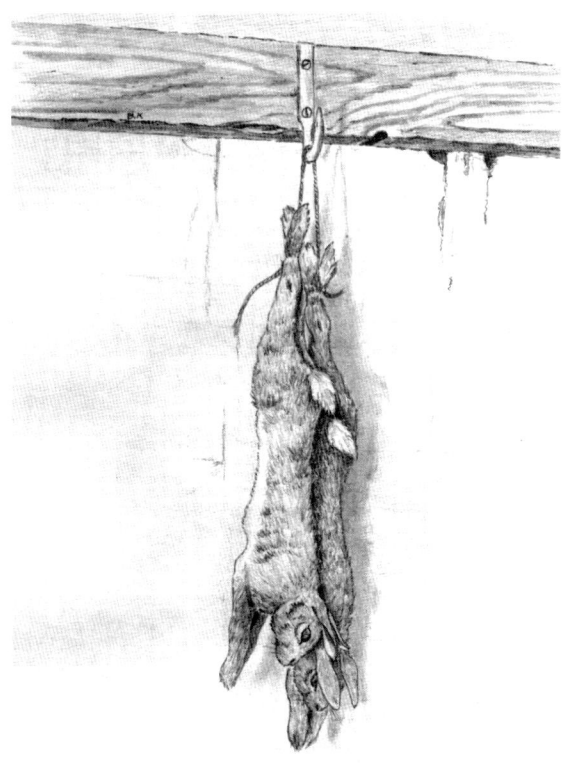

The cowshed meeting

Lightly Poached